The Wild Life of CATS

The Wild Life of CATS

A RUBES® CARTOON BOOK

BY LEIGH RUBIN

 WILLOW CREEK PRESS

For Sue and Dale and all of my cat-loving friends.

Published by Willow Creek Press
P.O. Box 147, Minocqua, Wisconsin 54548

Library of Congress Cataloging-in-Publication Data: On file

Printed in Canada

They're mysterious and fearless

Curious and courageous

Intriguing and enchanting

Captivating and cunning

Graceful and playful

Beautiful and agile

Treasured and revered

Worshiped and adored

Pampered and cuddled

But most of all, they're loved...

They're Cats!

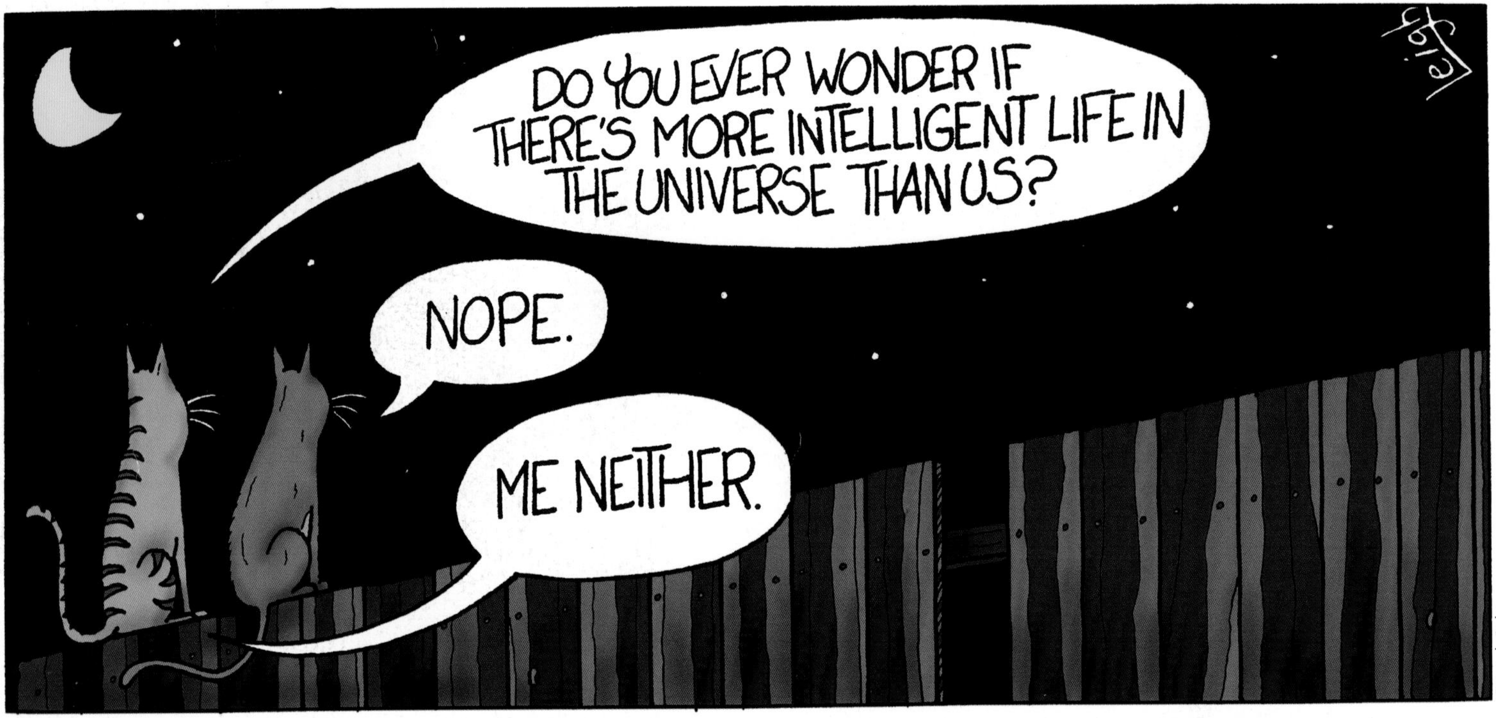
DO YOU EVER WONDER IF THERE'S MORE INTELLIGENT LIFE IN THE UNIVERSE THAN US?
NOPE.
ME NEITHER.
Leigh
© Leigh Rubin

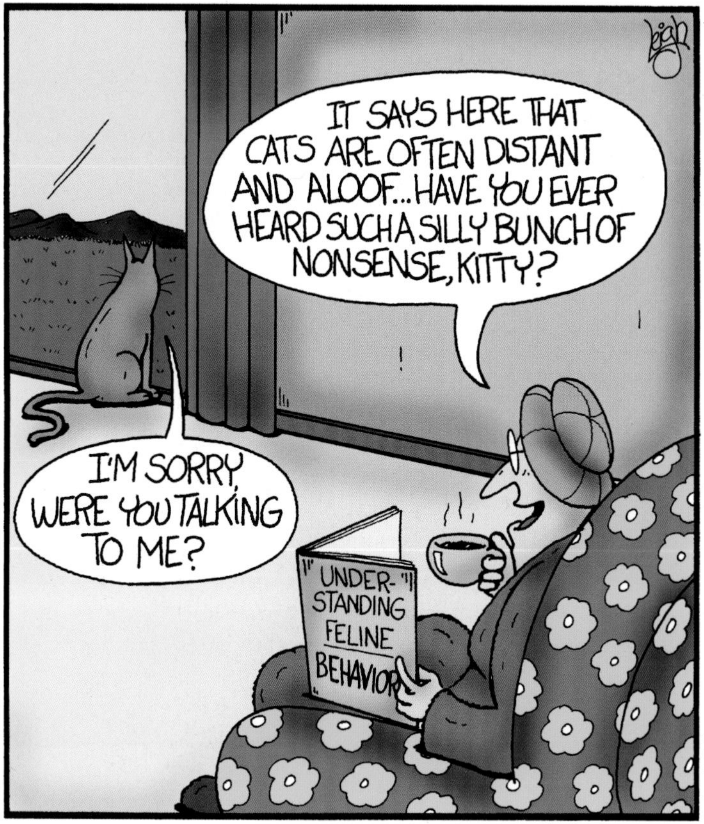
IT SAYS HERE THAT CATS ARE OFTEN DISTANT AND ALOOF...HAVE YOU EVER HEARD SUCH A SILLY BUNCH OF NONSENSE, KITTY?
I'M SORRY, WERE YOU TALKING TO ME?
UNDER-STANDING FELINE BEHAVIOR

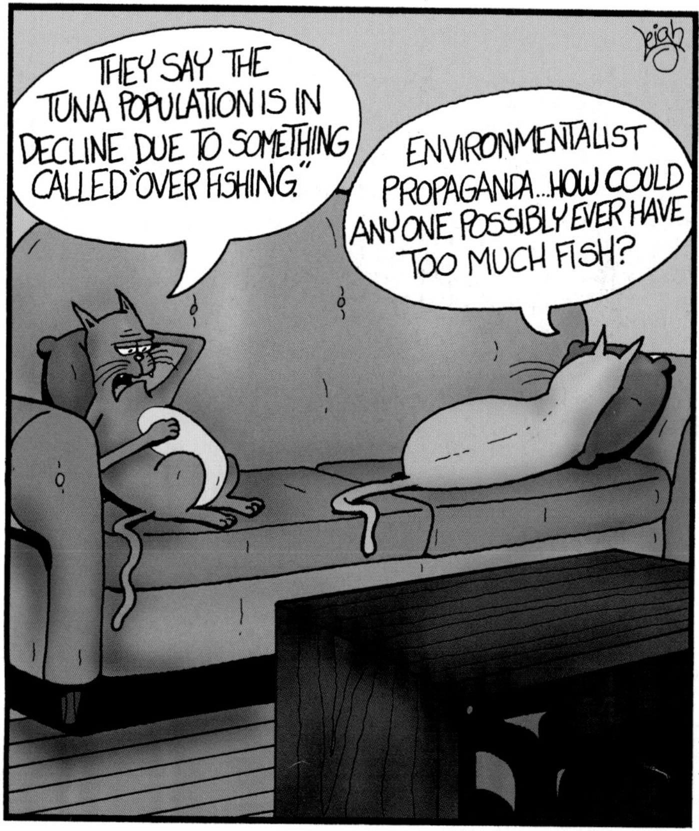
THEY SAY THE TUNA POPULATION IS IN DECLINE DUE TO SOMETHING CALLED "OVER FISHING."
ENVIRONMENTALIST PROPAGANDA...HOW COULD ANYONE POSSIBLY EVER HAVE TOO MUCH FISH?

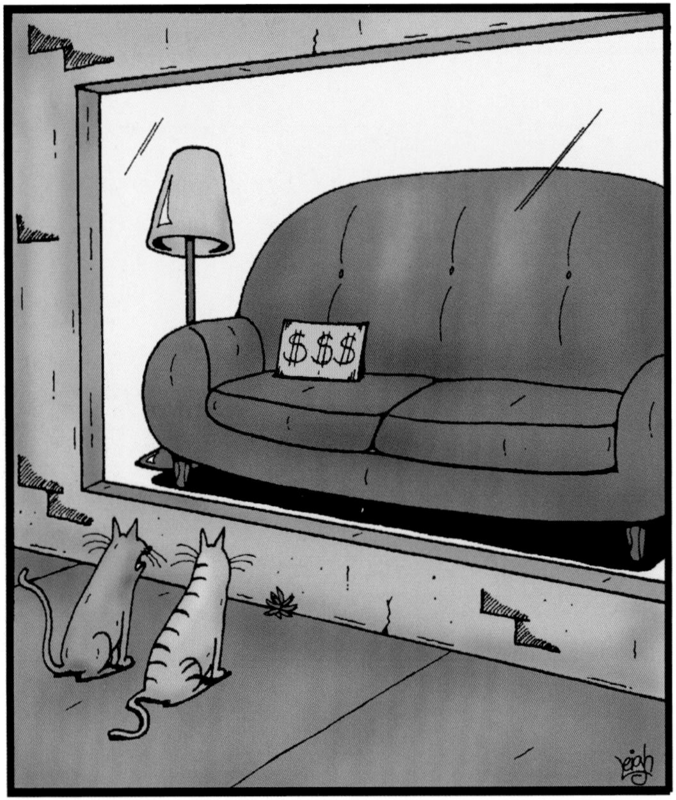
$$$
leigh

© Leigh Rubin

"A $3,000 genuine leather, four-legged scratching post ... I'm telling you, Maurice, the rich really *are* different from us."

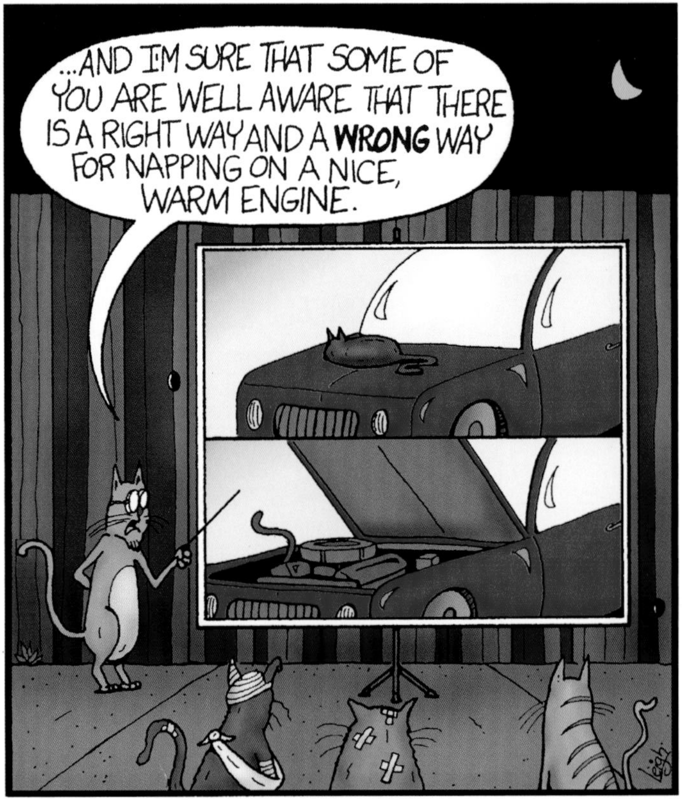
...AND I'M SURE THAT SOME OF YOU ARE WELL AWARE THAT THERE IS A RIGHT WAY AND A **WRONG** WAY FOR NAPPING ON A NICE, WARM ENGINE.
leigh

© Leigh Rubin

Automotive safety class for cats

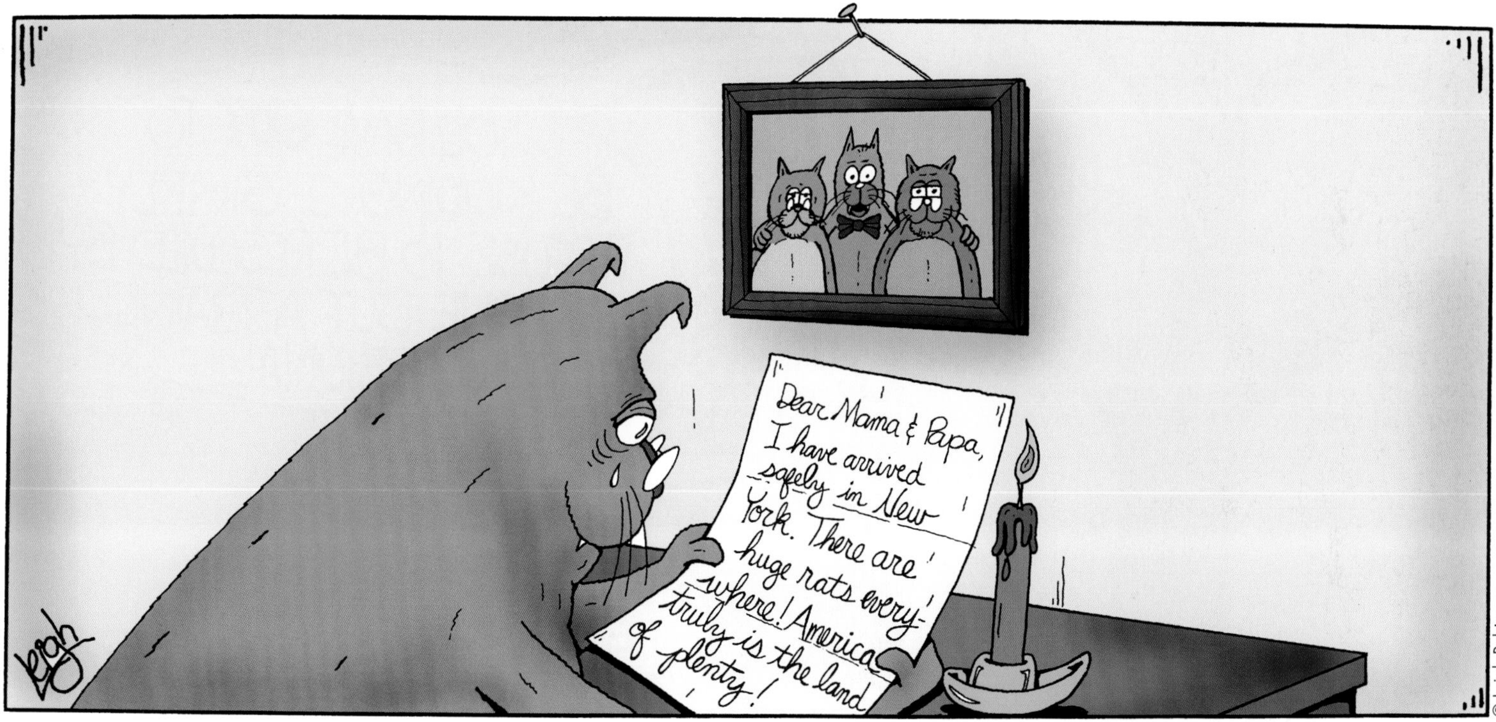
Dear Mama & Papa,
I have arrived safely in New York. There are huge rats every-where! America truly is the land of plenty!

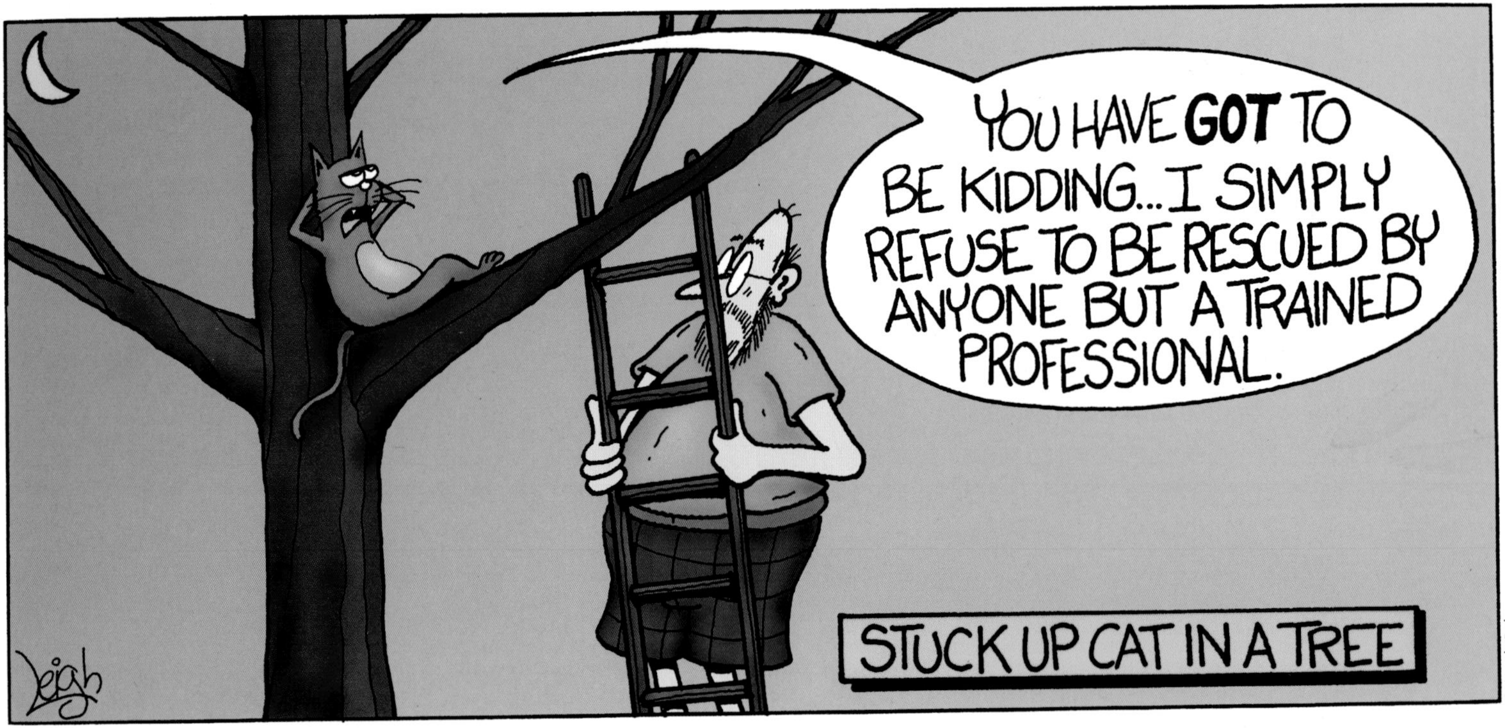
YOU HAVE **GOT** TO BE KIDDING...I SIMPLY REFUSE TO BE RESCUED BY ANYONE BUT A TRAINED PROFESSIONAL.
STUCK UP CAT IN A TREE
Leigh

© Leigh Rubin

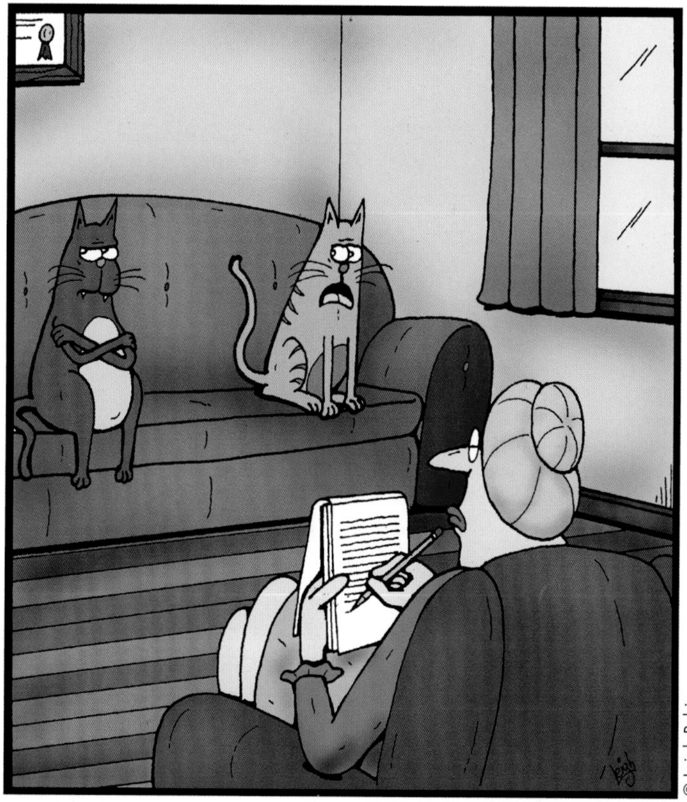
leigh

"It's our love life, Doc. She never feels, well, you know ... *frisky*."

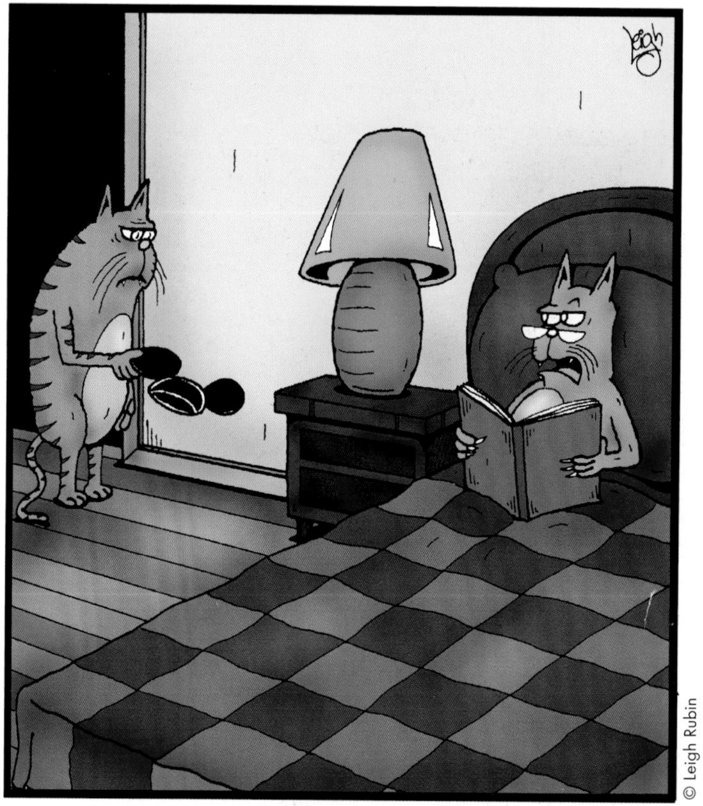
leigh

"No, Sidney, for the last time, I will *not* put that silly thing on and let you chase me around the house!"

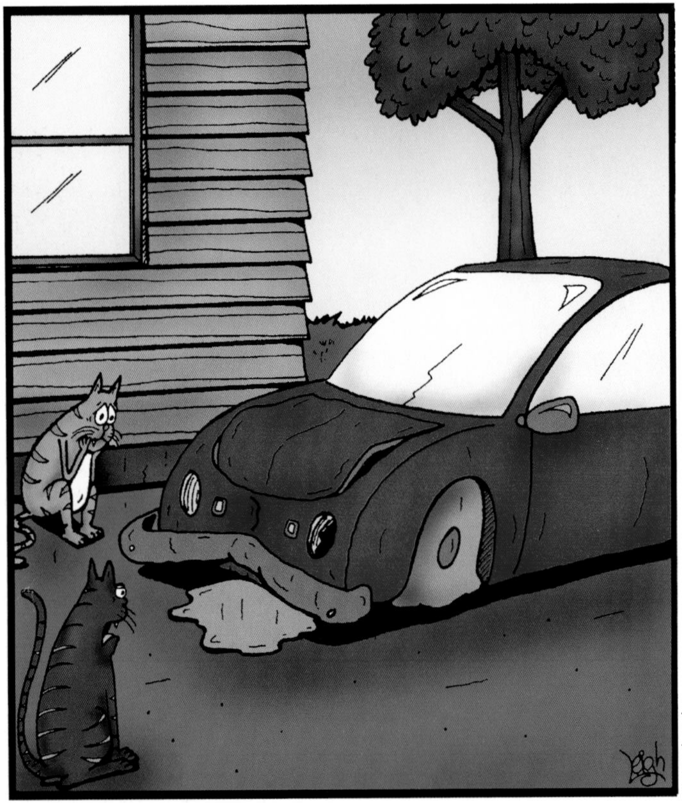

"Wow, I wouldn't want to be around when your father sees this. All I can say is, it's a good thing you have *nine* lives."

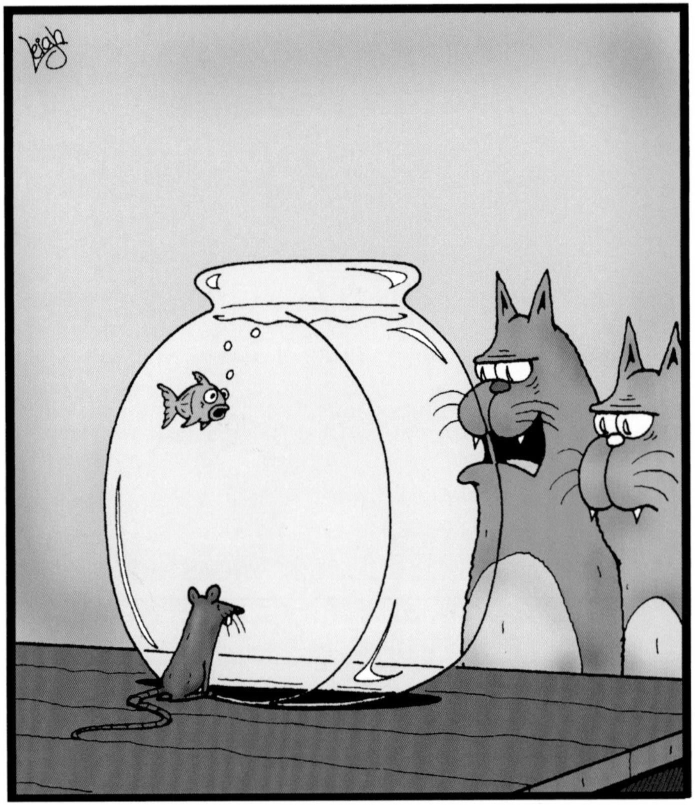

"I don't know how he can possibly hold his breath for so long, but you can rest assured that when he comes up for air, I'll be waiting for him."

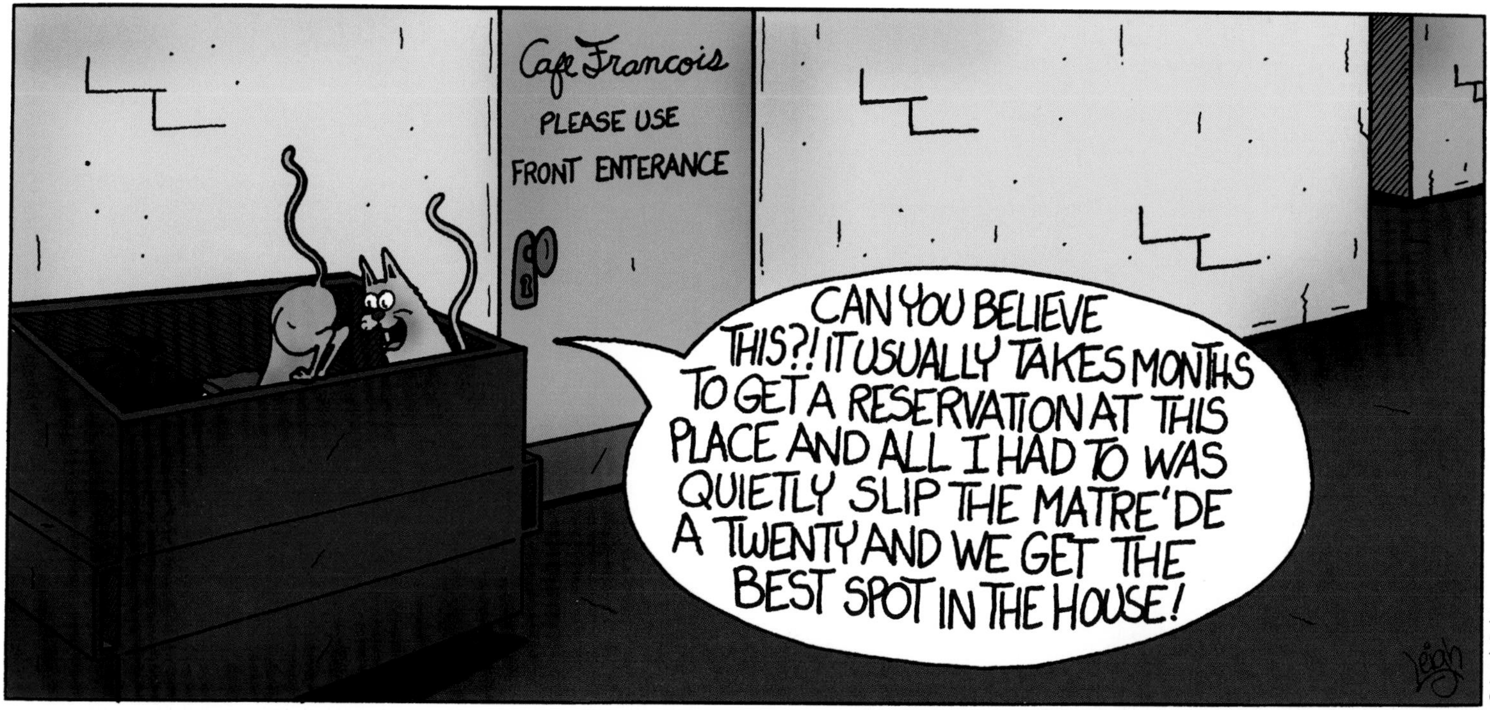
Cafe Francois
PLEASE USE
FRONT ENTERANCE
CAN YOU BELIEVE THIS?! IT USUALLY TAKES MONTHS TO GET A RESERVATION AT THIS PLACE AND ALL I HAD TO WAS QUIETLY SLIP THE MATRE'DE A TWENTY AND WE GET THE BEST SPOT IN THE HOUSE!
Leigh

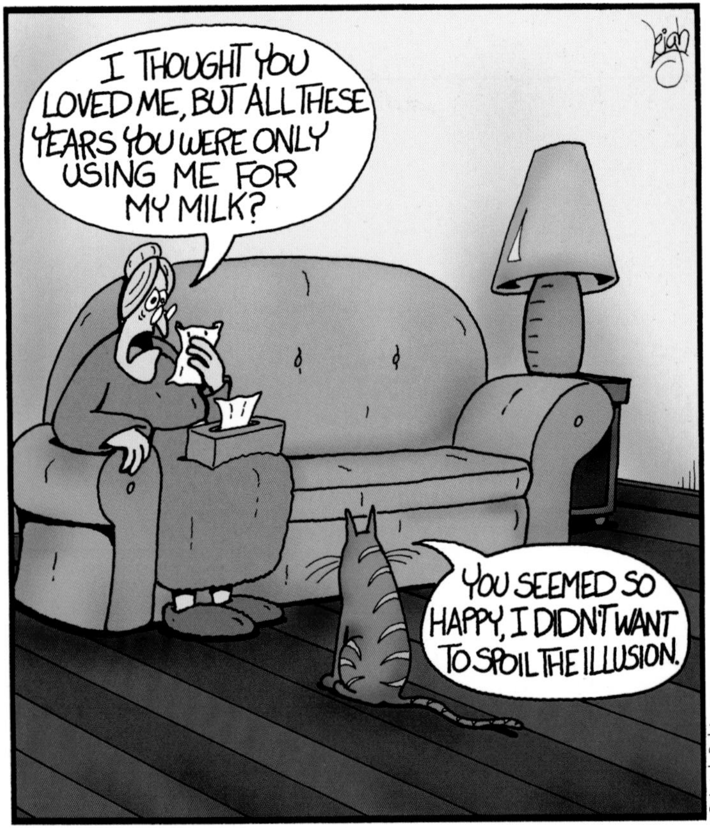
I THOUGHT YOU LOVED ME, BUT ALL THESE YEARS YOU WERE ONLY USING ME FOR MY MILK?
YOU SEEMED SO HAPPY, I DIDN'T WANT TO SPOIL THE ILLUSION.
leigh

© Leigh Rubin

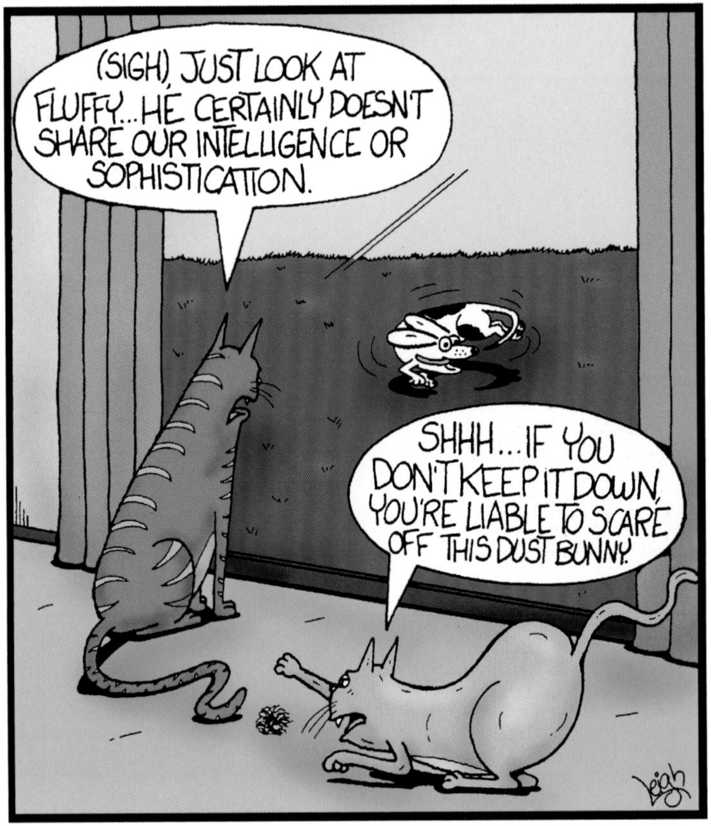
(SIGH), JUST LOOK AT FLUFFY... HE CERTAINLY DOESN'T SHARE OUR INTELLIGENCE OR SOPHISTICATION.
SHHH... IF YOU DON'T KEEP IT DOWN, YOU'RE LIABLE TO SCARE OFF THIS DUST BUNNY.
leigh

© Leigh Rubin

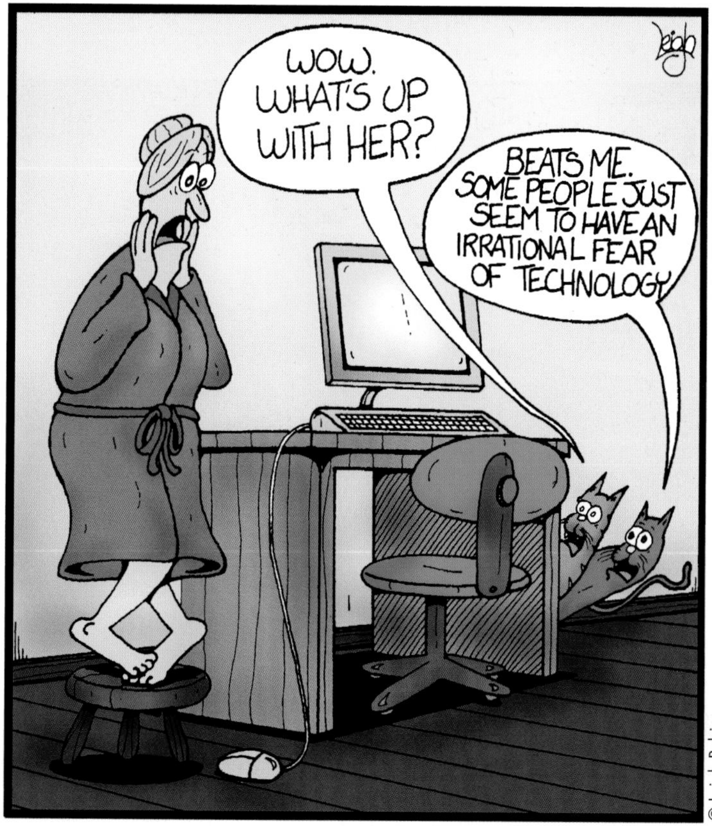
WOW. WHAT'S UP WITH HER?
BEATS ME. SOME PEOPLE JUST SEEM TO HAVE AN IRRATIONAL FEAR OF TECHNOLOGY.
Leigh

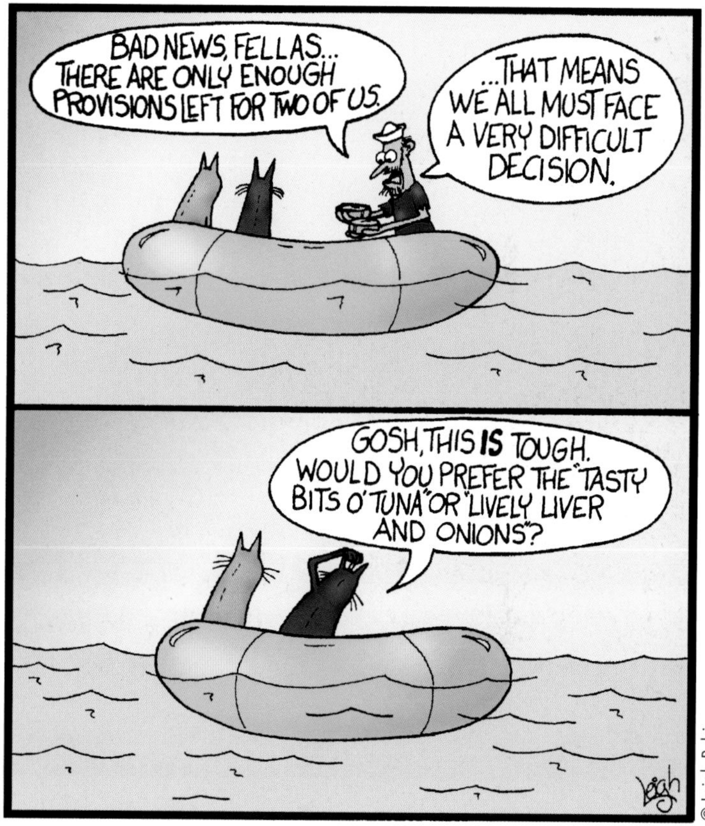
BAD NEWS, FELLAS... THERE ARE ONLY ENOUGH PROVISIONS LEFT FOR TWO OF US.
...THAT MEANS WE ALL MUST FACE A VERY DIFFICULT DECISION.
GOSH, THIS **IS** TOUGH. WOULD YOU PREFER THE "TASTY BITS O' TUNA" OR "LIVELY LIVER AND ONIONS"?
Leigh

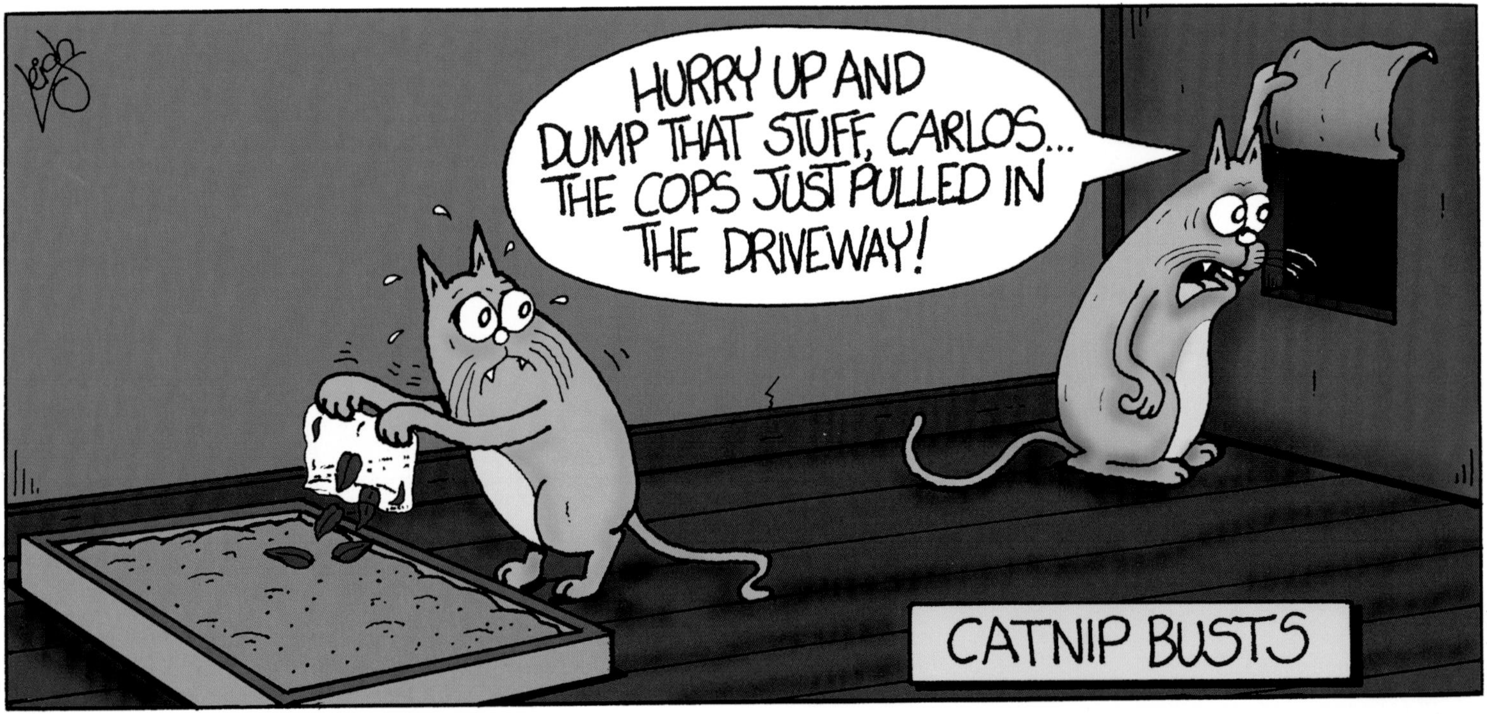
HURRY UP AND DUMP THAT STUFF, CARLOS... THE COPS JUST PULLED IN THE DRIVEWAY!
CATNIP BUSTS

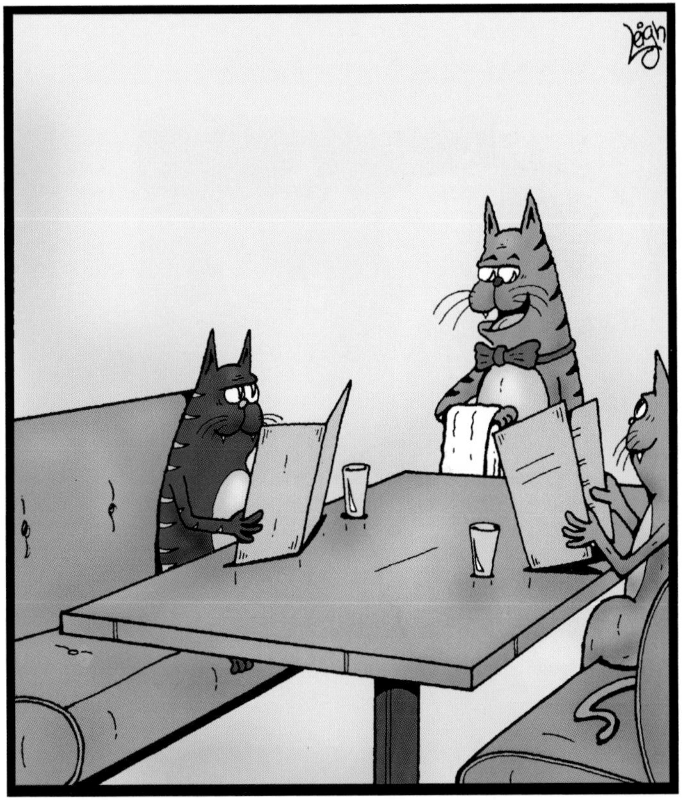
Leigh

"Perhaps I could interest you folks in our catch of the day? ... A fresh garden-variety gopher lightly batted around to perfection."

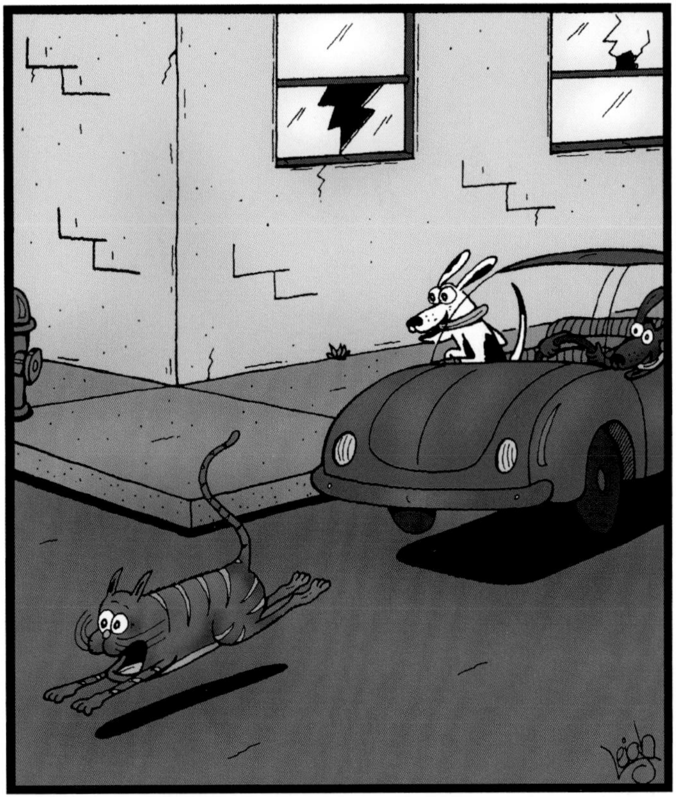
Leigh

Another reason not to leave dogs unattended in your car.

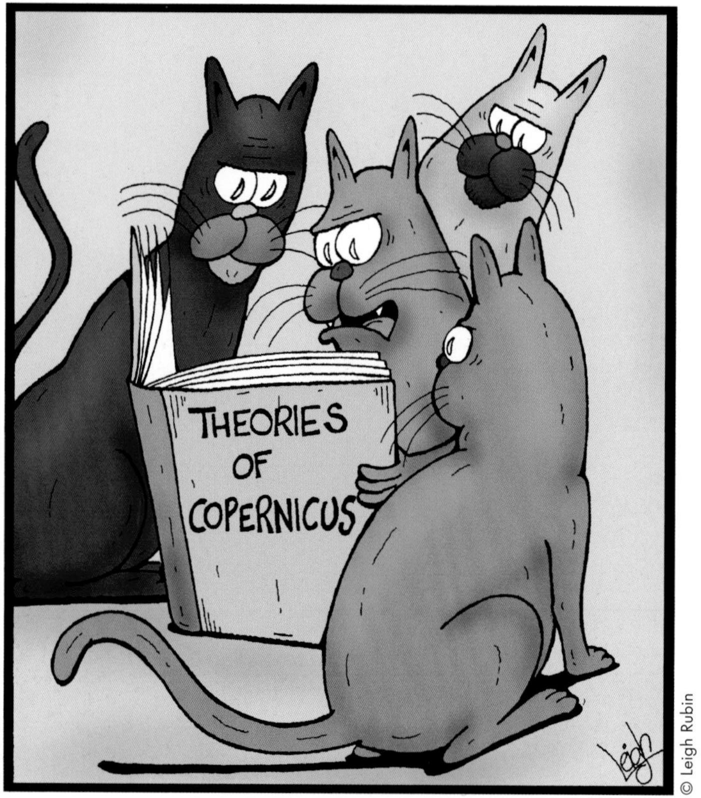
THEORIES
OF
COPERNICUS
© Leigh Rubin

"This is pure heresy! Everybody knows that the Earth revolves around *us*!"

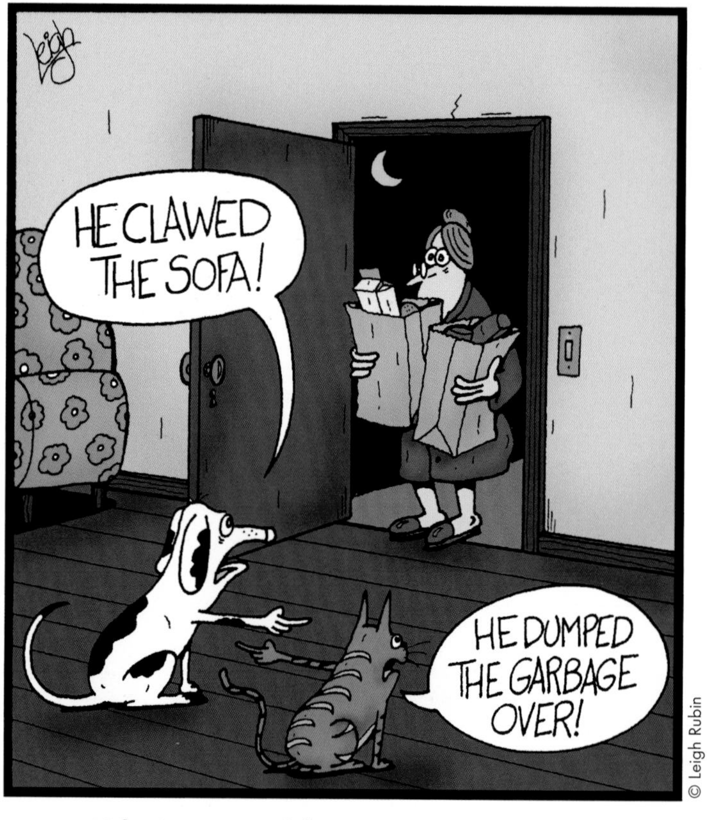
HE CLAWED THE SOFA!
HE DUMPED THE GARBAGE OVER!
© Leigh Rubin

Why it's a good thing our pets can't talk.

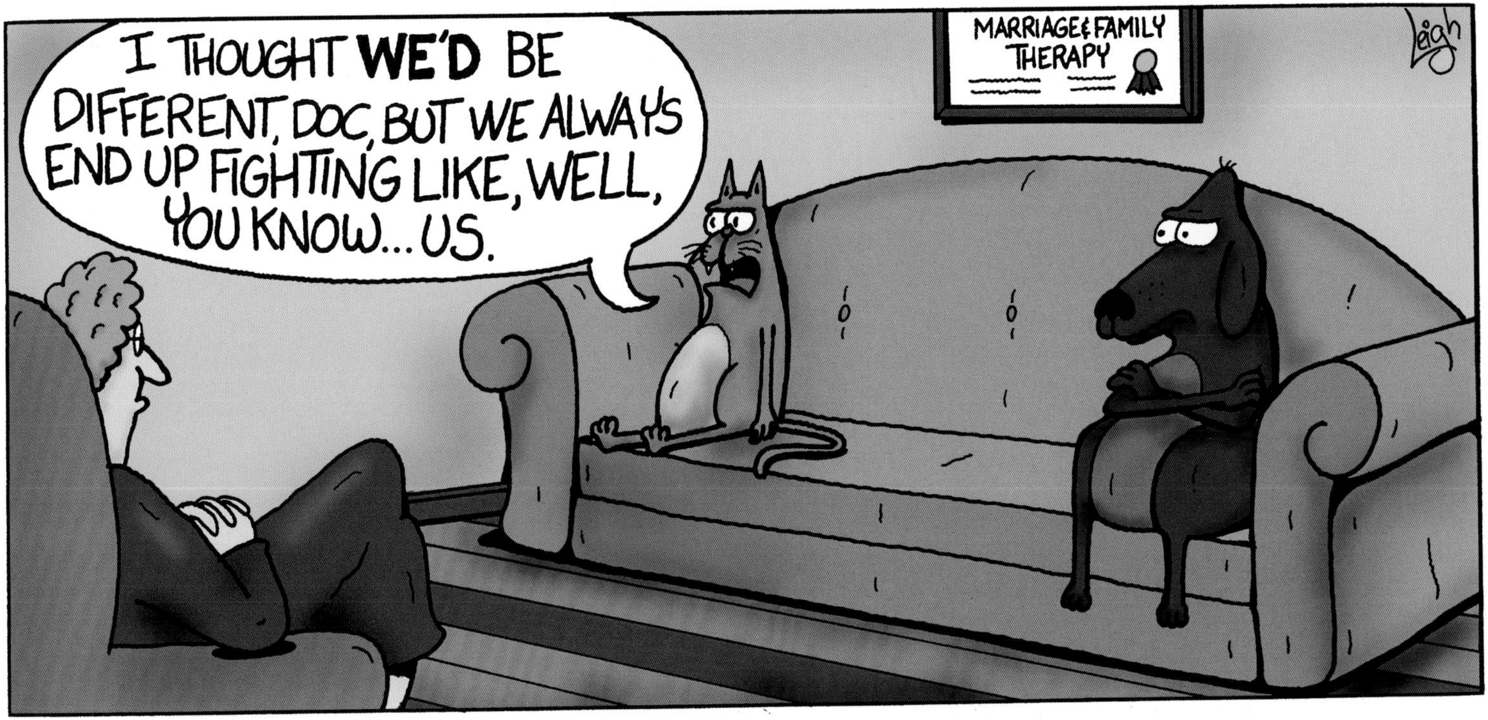
I THOUGHT WE'D BE DIFFERENT, DOC, BUT WE ALWAYS END UP FIGHTING LIKE, WELL, YOU KNOW... US.
MARRIAGE & FAMILY THERAPY
Leigh

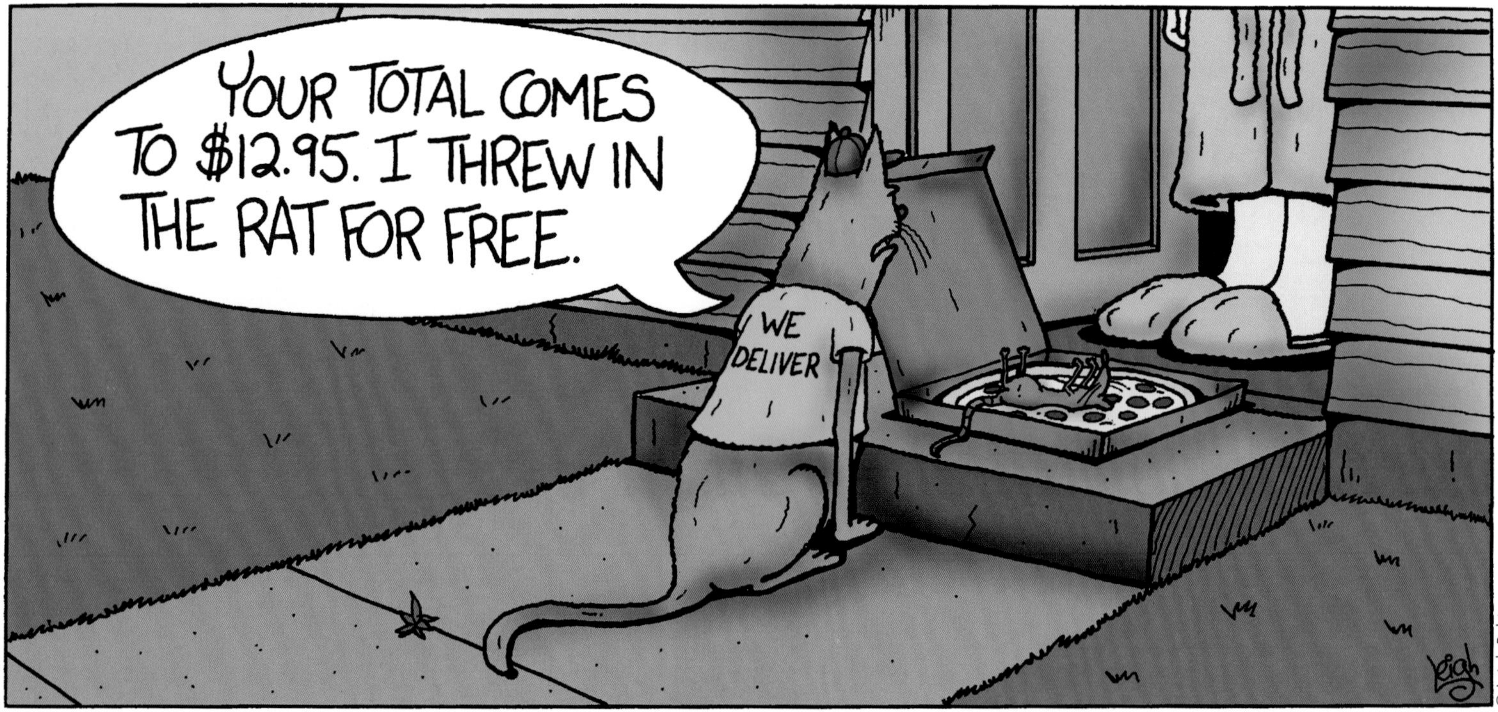
YOUR TOTAL COMES TO $12.95. I THREW IN THE RAT FOR FREE.
WE DELIVER
Leigh

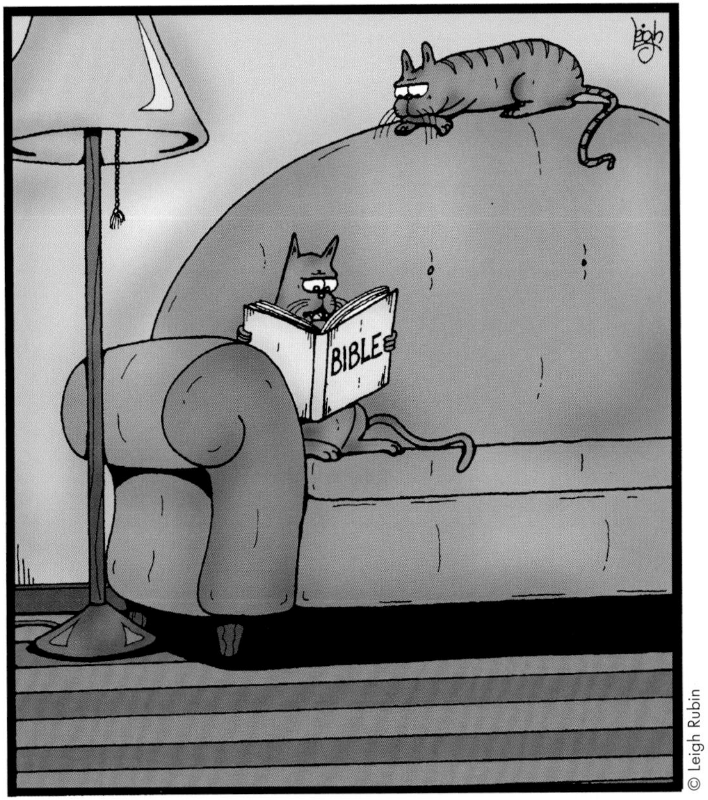

BIBLE
© Leigh Rubin

"Well, I can't find any reference that confirms or refutes that all dogs go to heaven, but assuming it's true, that certainly doesn't provide us with much motivation to behave."

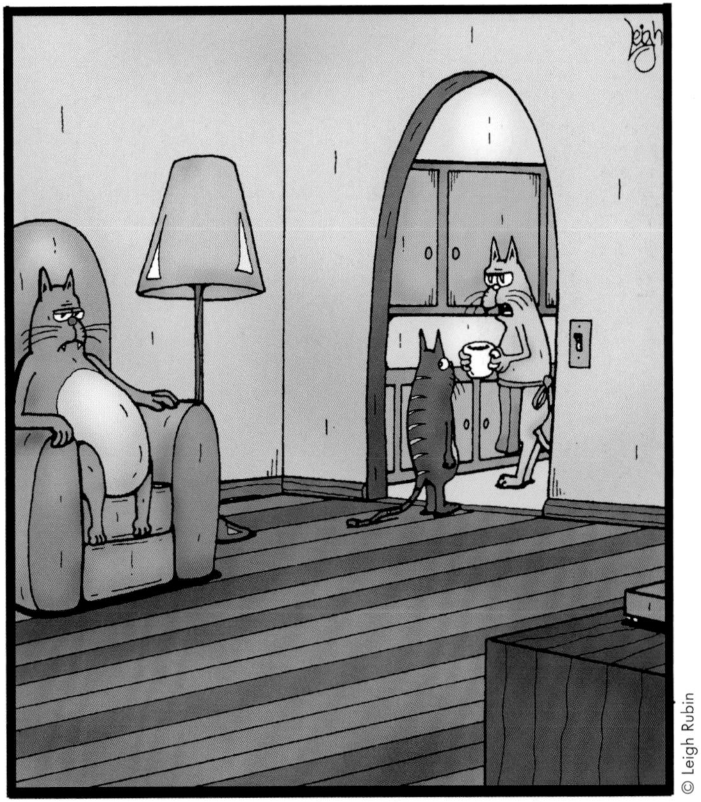

© Leigh Rubin

"Yes, son, it's true. Our whiskers are roughly the same width as our body and are primarily used to see if we can fit through an opening. There are, however, exceptions to the rule."

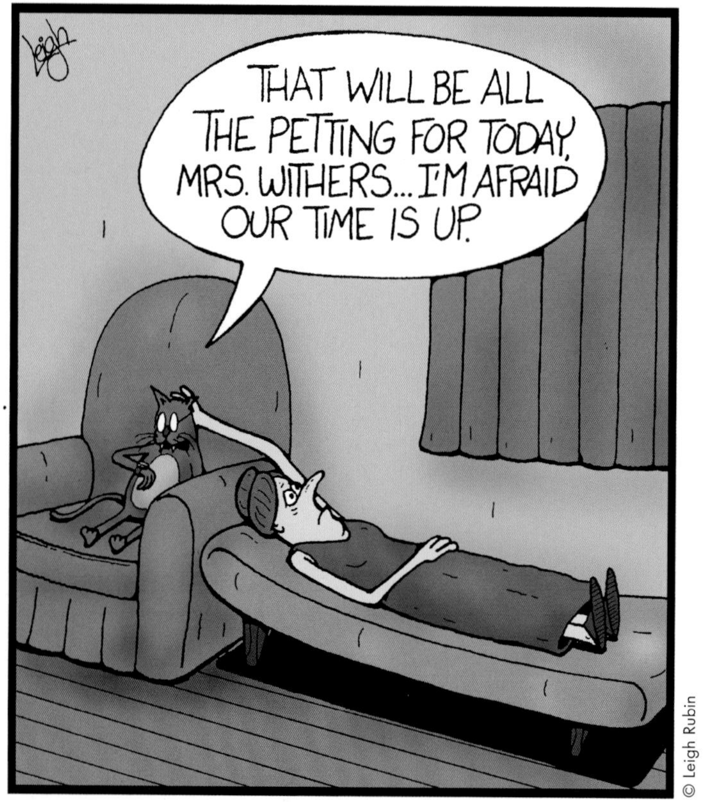
THAT WILL BE ALL THE PETTING FOR TODAY, MRS. WITHERS... I'M AFRAID OUR TIME IS UP.
leigh
© Leigh Rubin

Pet therapy

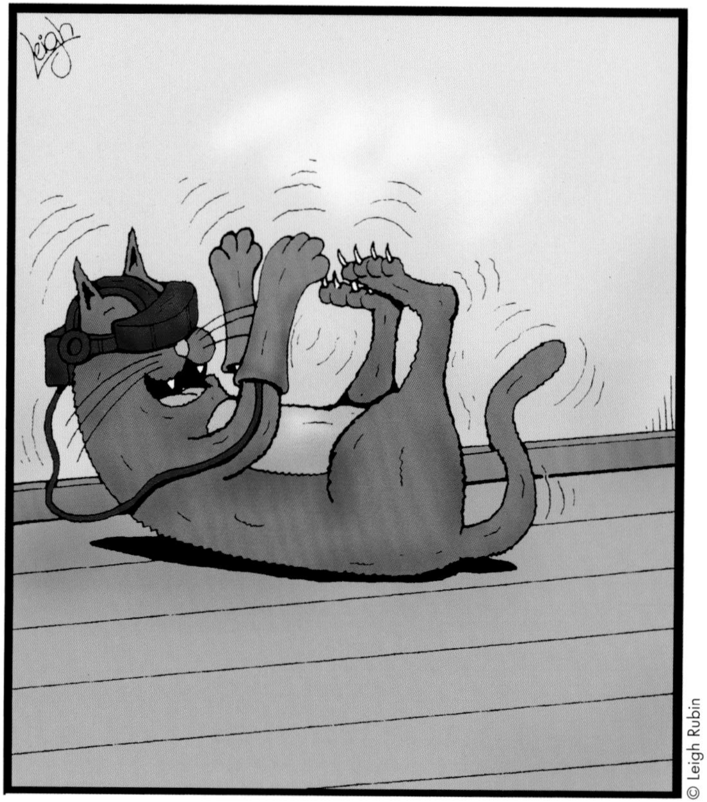
leigh
© Leigh Rubin

A favorite of high-tech kittens ... virtual ball of yarn

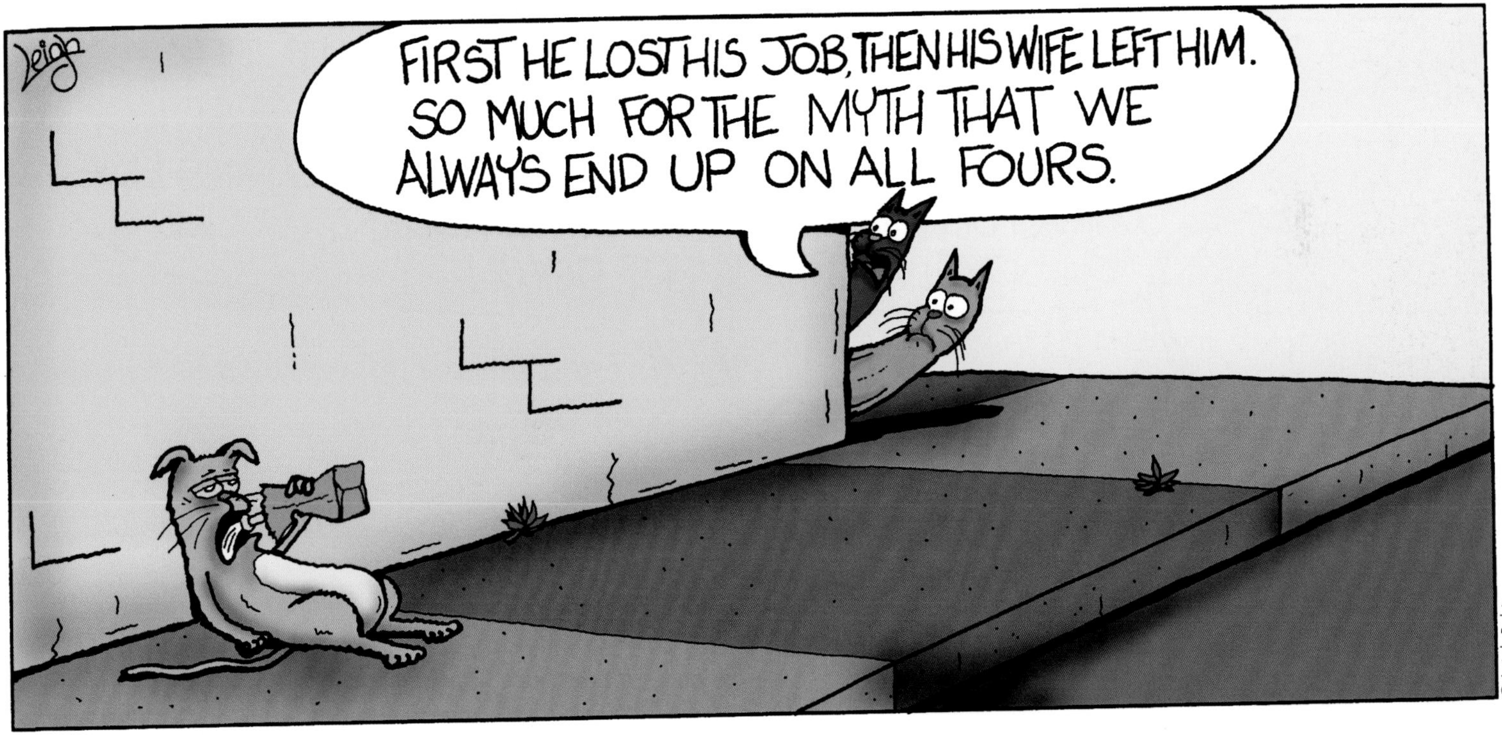
FIRST HE LOST HIS JOB, THEN HIS WIFE LEFT HIM. SO MUCH FOR THE MYTH THAT WE ALWAYS END UP ON ALL FOURS.
Leigh

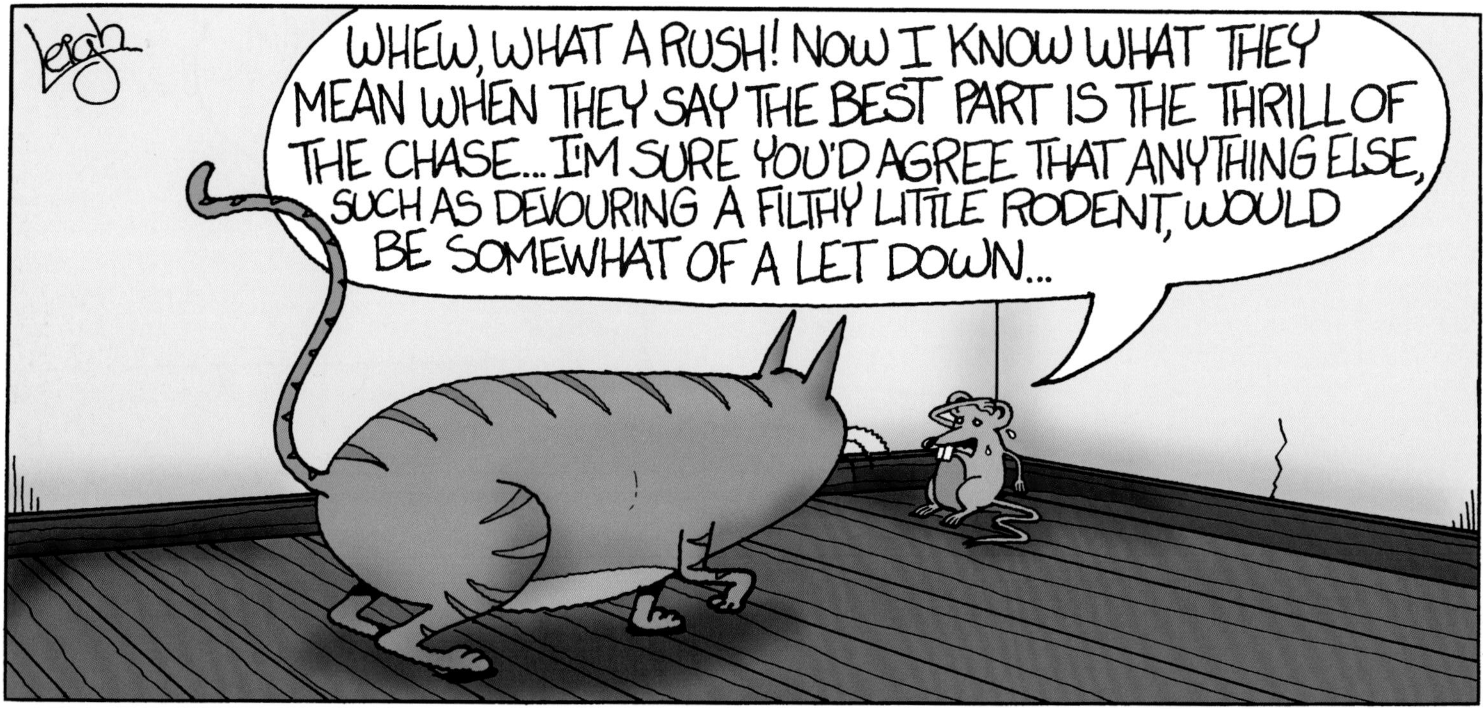
WHEW, WHAT A RUSH! NOW I KNOW WHAT THEY MEAN WHEN THEY SAY THE BEST PART IS THE THRILL OF THE CHASE... I'M SURE YOU'D AGREE THAT ANYTHING ELSE, SUCH AS DEVOURING A FILTHY LITTLE RODENT, WOULD BE SOMEWHAT OF A LET DOWN...
Leigh

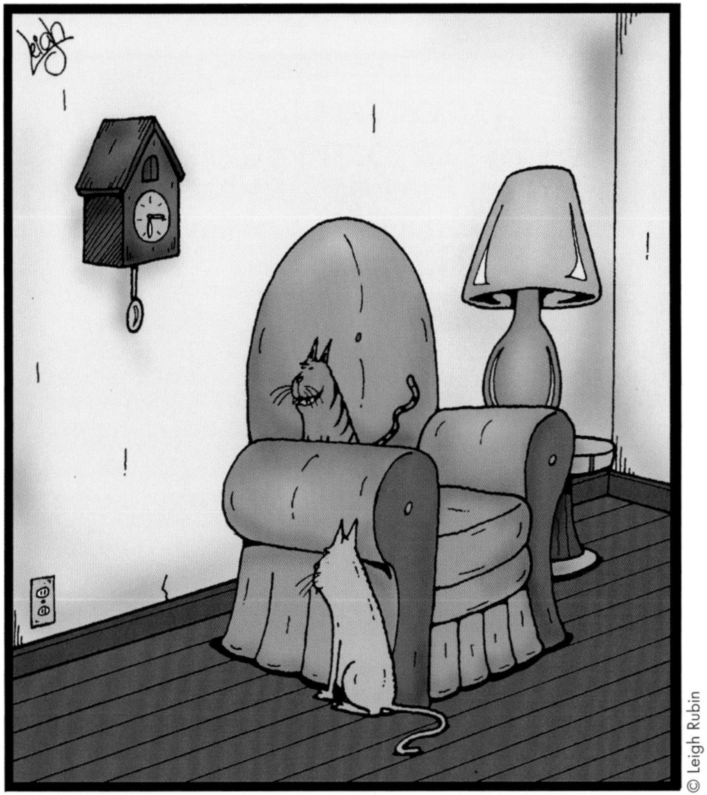

© Leigh Rubin

"Catching this guy oughta be a cinch. I've been studying his daily routine. He pops out of that hole every hour on the hour just like clockwork."

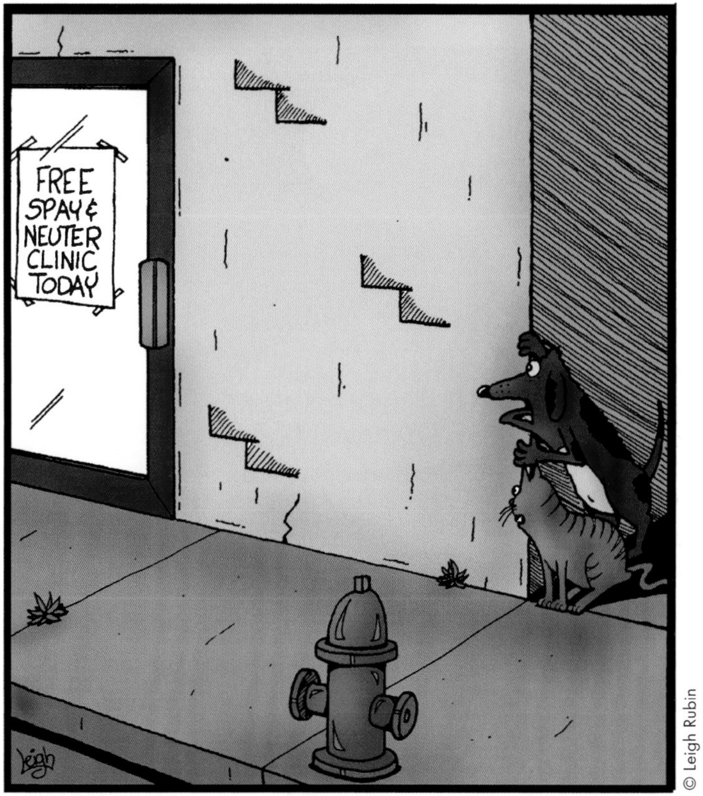

FREE
SPAY &
NEUTER
CLINIC
TODAY
© Leigh Rubin

"It's positively horrifying! How can they possibly promote such barbaric practices and still have the nerve to call themselves the *Humane* Society?"

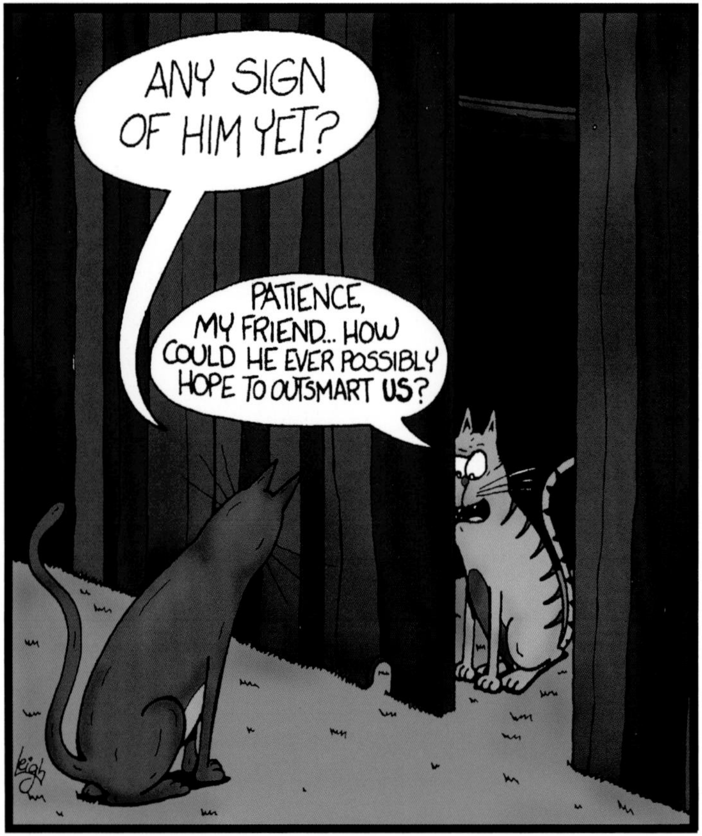
ANY SIGN OF HIM YET?
PATIENCE, MY FRIEND... HOW COULD HE EVER POSSIBLY HOPE TO OUTSMART US?
leigh

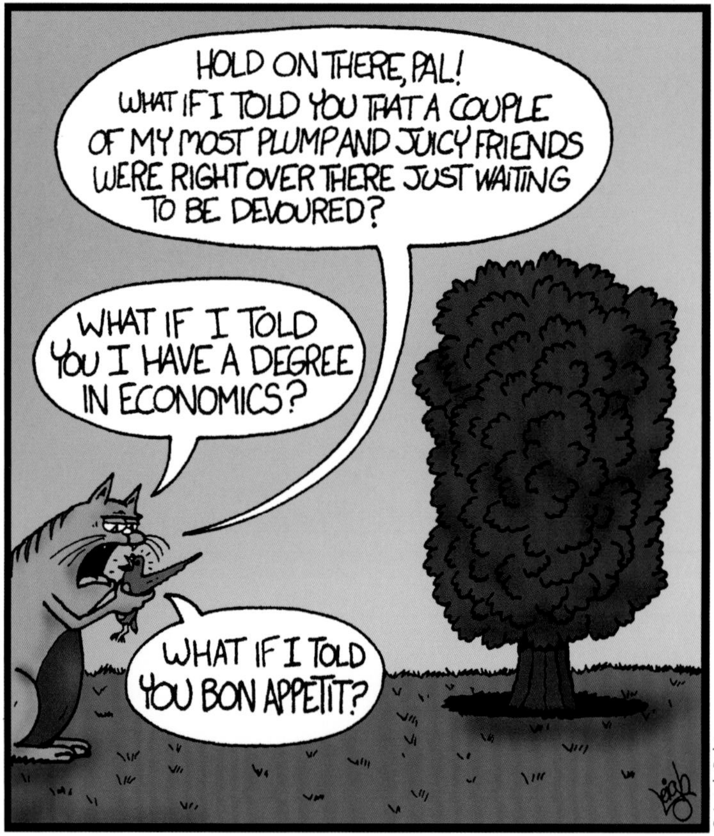
HOLD ON THERE, PAL! WHAT IF I TOLD YOU THAT A COUPLE OF MY MOST PLUMP AND JUICY FRIENDS WERE RIGHT OVER THERE JUST WAITING TO BE DEVOURED?
WHAT IF I TOLD YOU I HAVE A DEGREE IN ECONOMICS?
WHAT IF I TOLD YOU BON APPETIT?
leigh

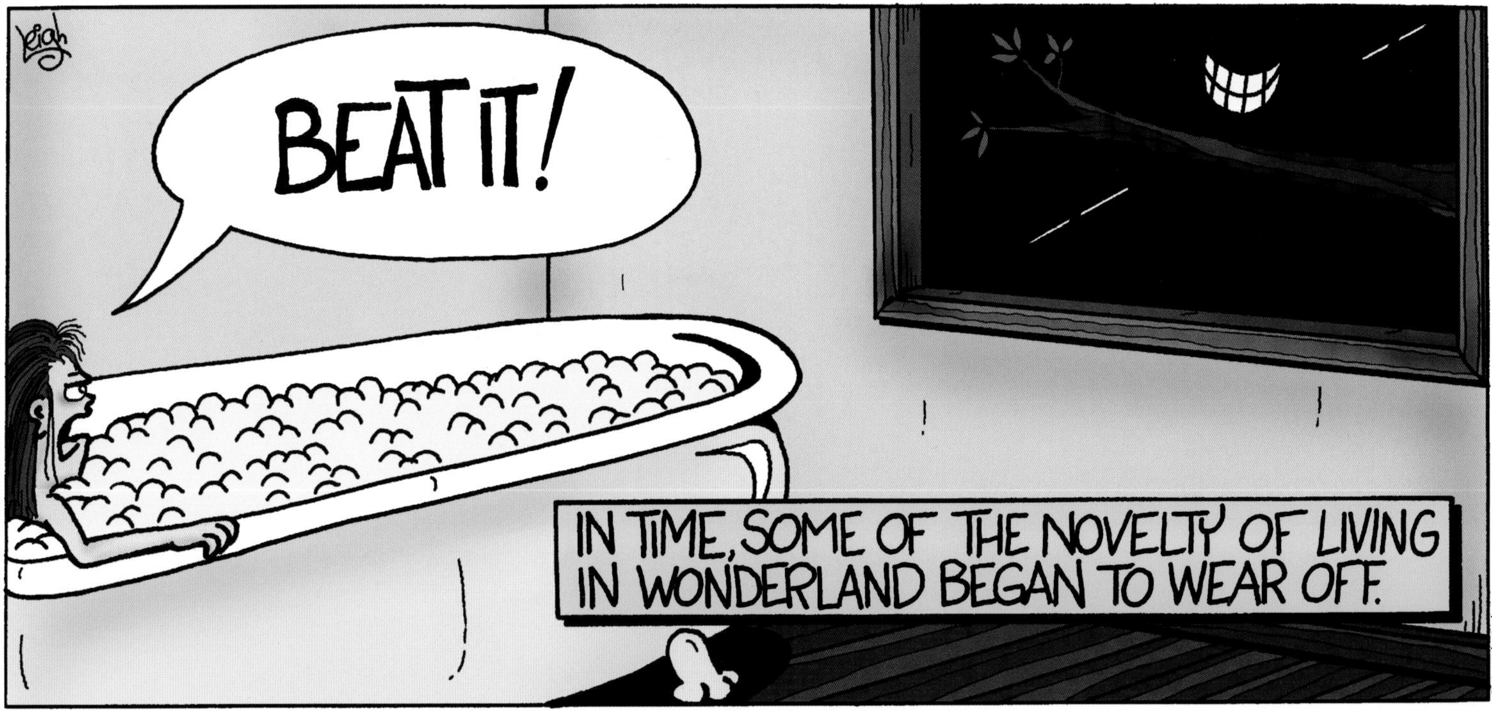

Leigh
BEAT IT!
IN TIME, SOME OF THE NOVELTY OF LIVING IN WONDERLAND BEGAN TO WEAR OFF.

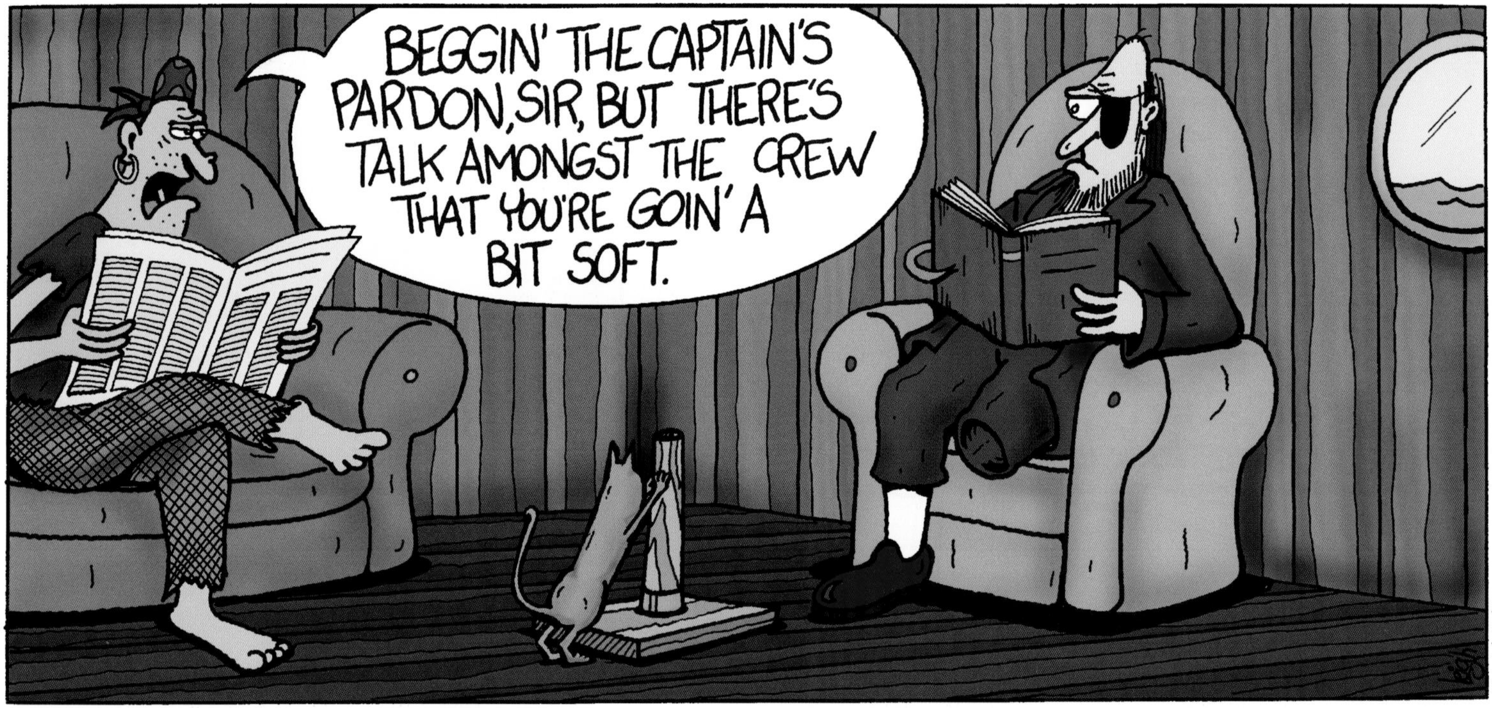
BEGGIN' THE CAPTAIN'S PARDON, SIR, BUT THERE'S TALK AMONGST THE CREW THAT YOU'RE GOIN' A BIT SOFT.

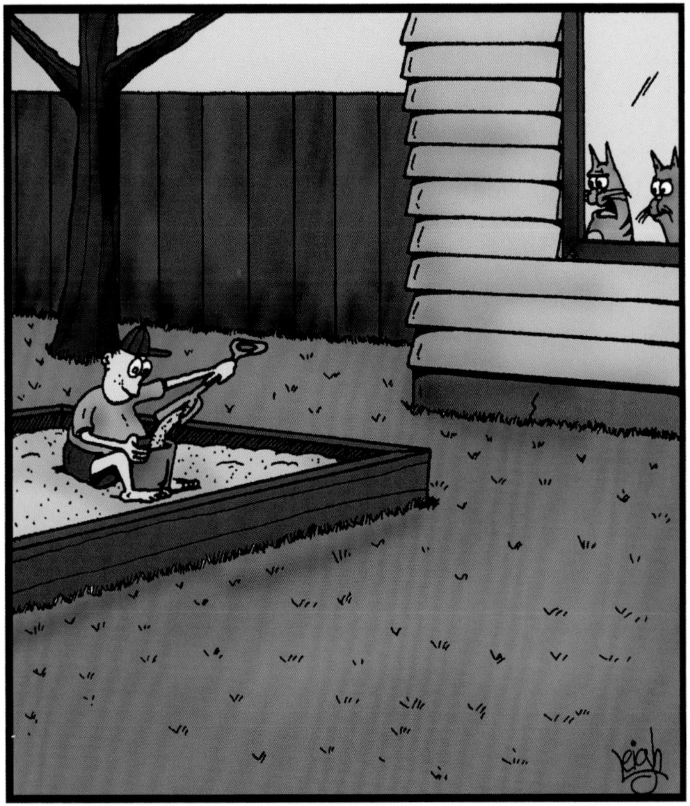

leigh

© Leigh Rubin

"Of all the disgusting things! ... What parent in their right mind would permit their child to play in *our* toilet?!"

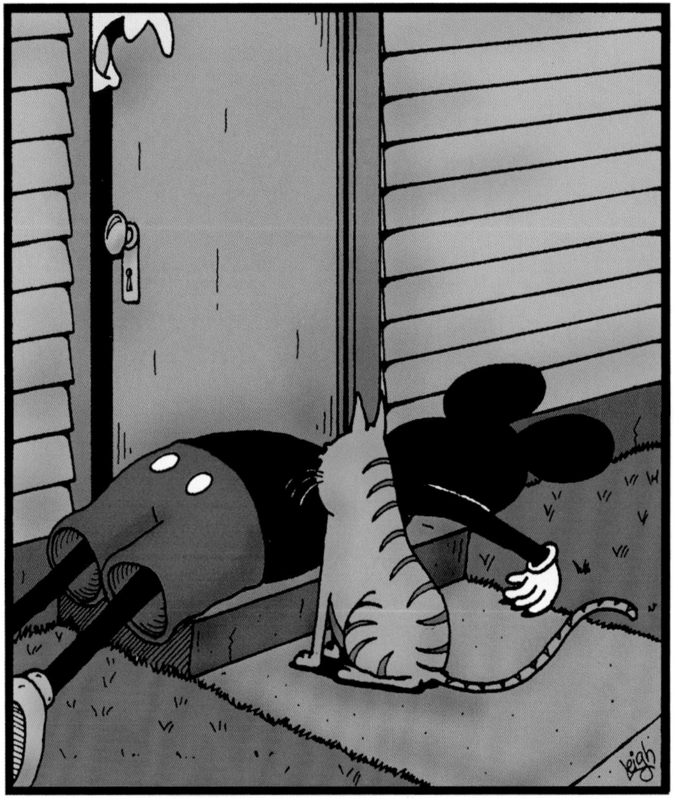

leigh

© Leigh Rubin

"Come look, honey. Muffy brought us back a little gift from Orlando."

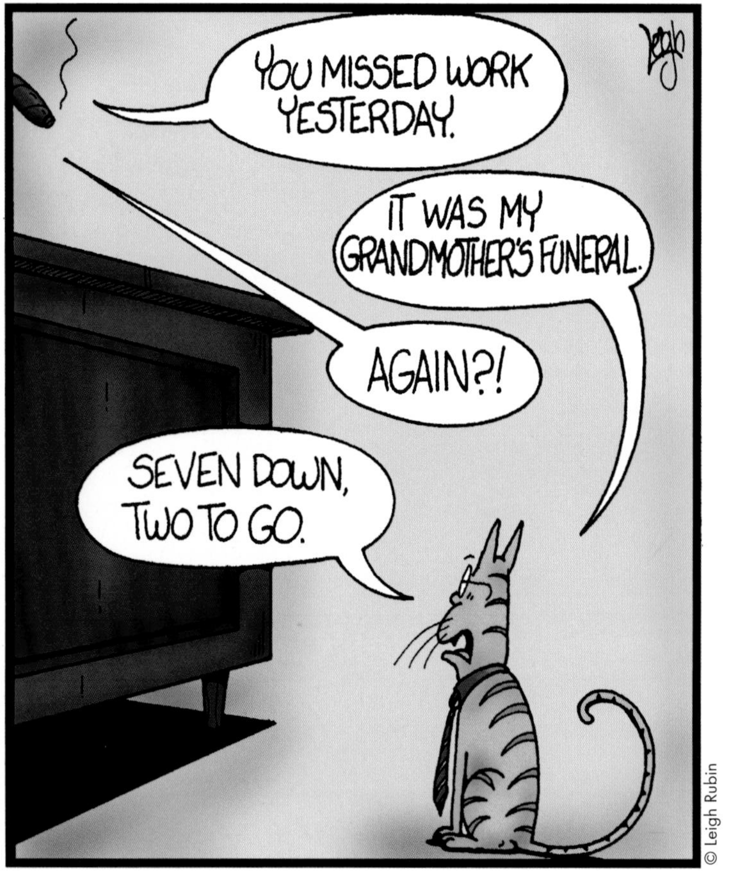
YOU MISSED WORK YESTERDAY.
IT WAS MY GRANDMOTHER'S FUNERAL.
AGAIN?!
SEVEN DOWN, TWO TO GO.
© Leigh Rubin

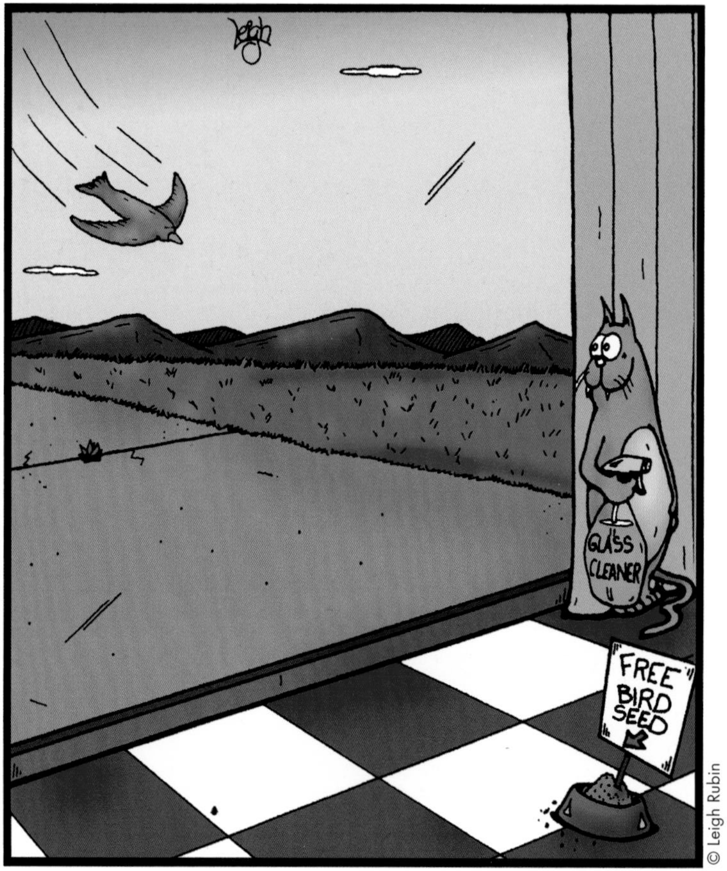
GLASS CLEANER
FREE BIRD SEED
© Leigh Rubin

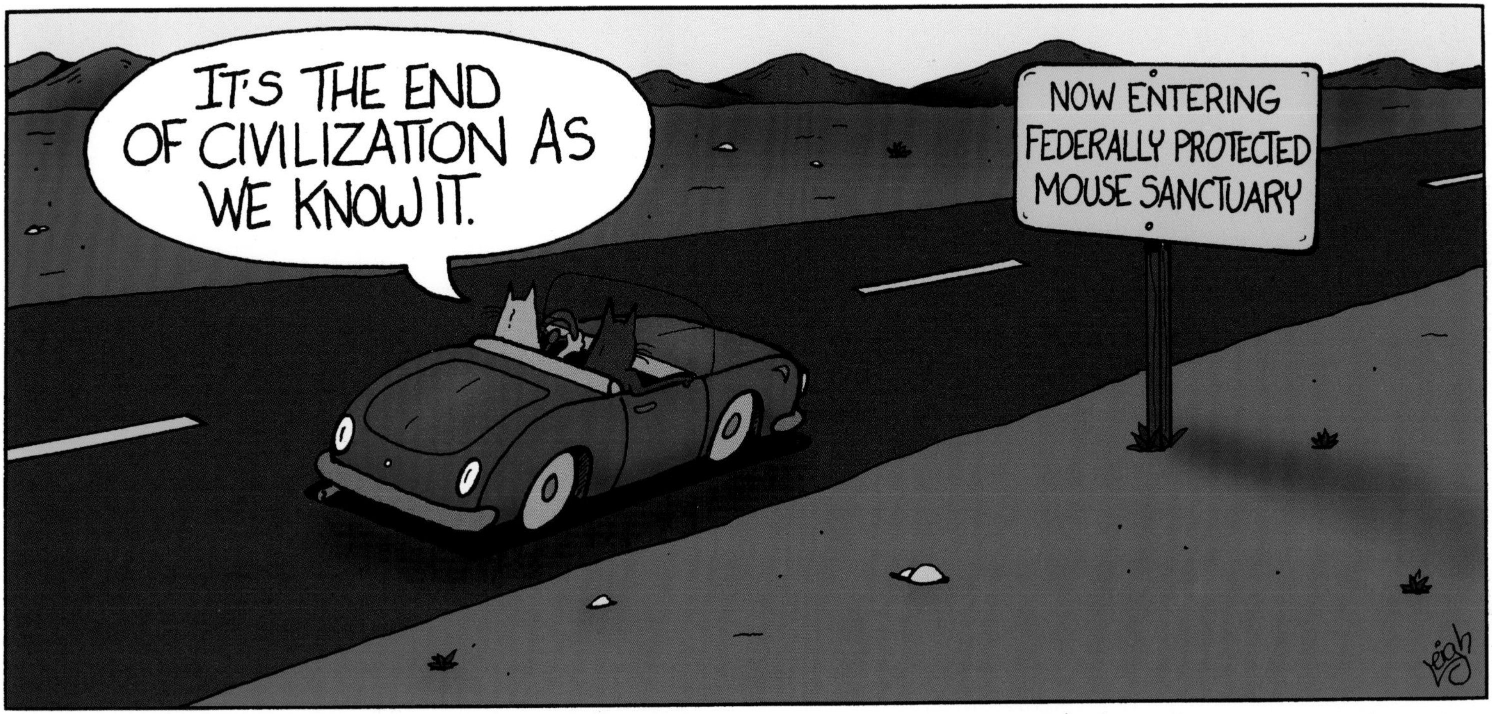
IT'S THE END OF CIVILIZATION AS WE KNOW IT.
NOW ENTERING FEDERALLY PROTECTED MOUSE SANCTUARY
leigh

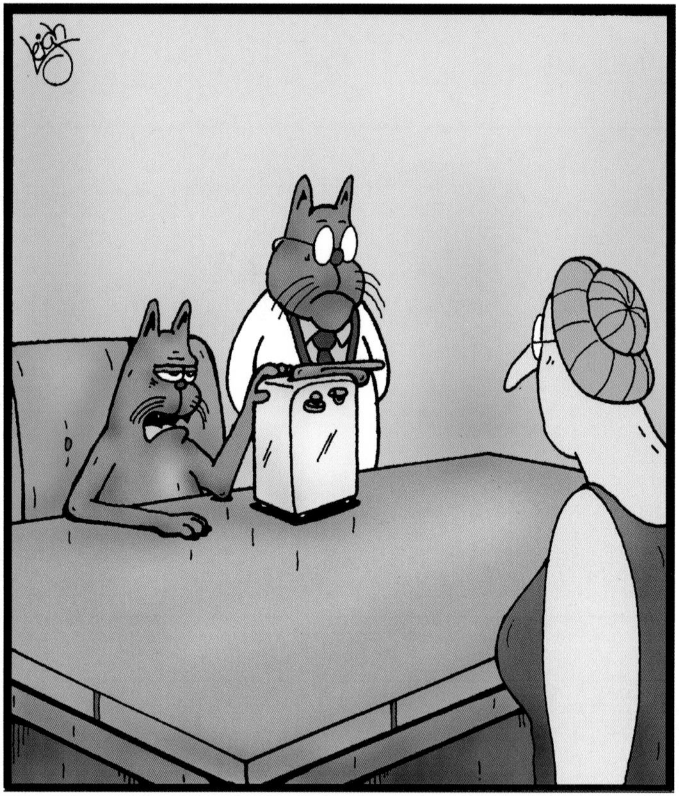

© Leigh Rubin

"Now that we've figured out how to operate this little device of yours, Mrs. Sugarman, your services will no longer be necessary."

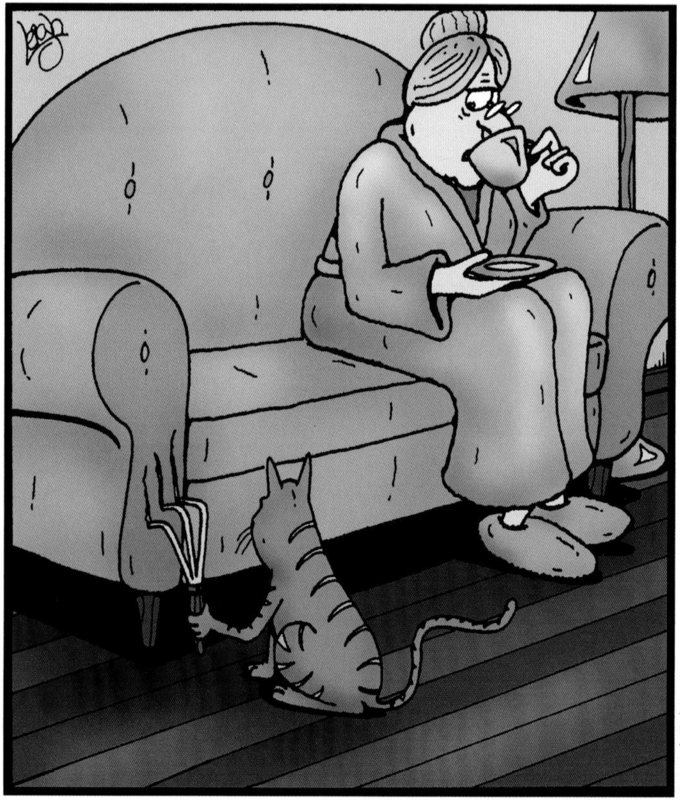

© Leigh Rubin

Apparently, Cleo's declawing failed to produce the desired result.

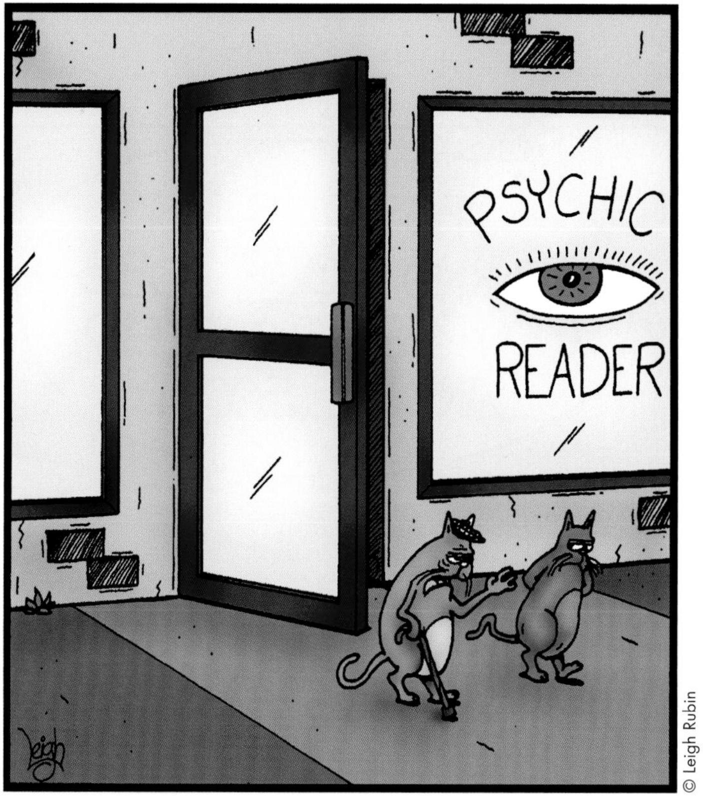
PSYCHIC
READER
leigh
© Leigh Rubin

"She said in my last eight lives I was a cat ... Phooey! I didn't need to pay fifty bucks for someone to tell me that!"

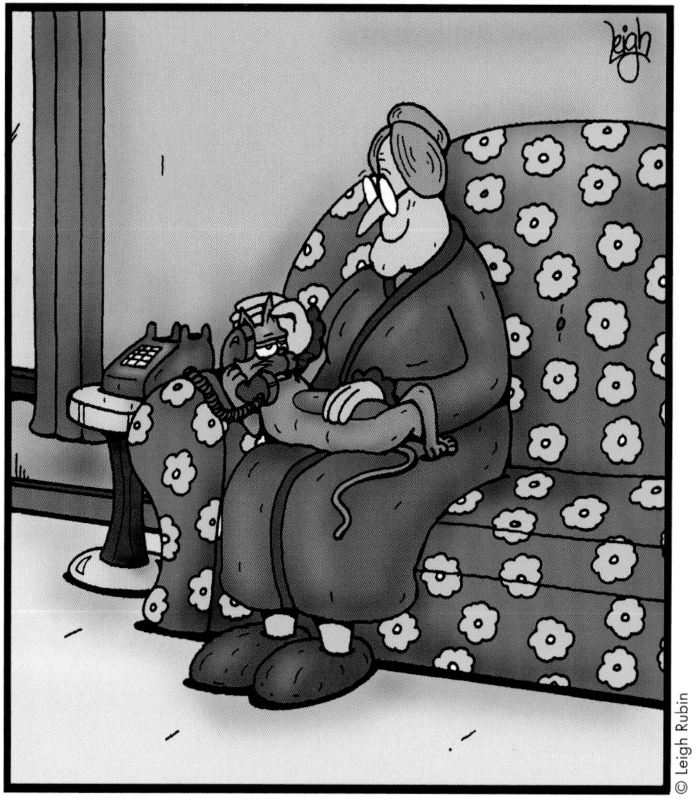
leigh
© Leigh Rubin

"Hey, listen, can I call you back? I'm not quite done receiving my morning quota of adoration."

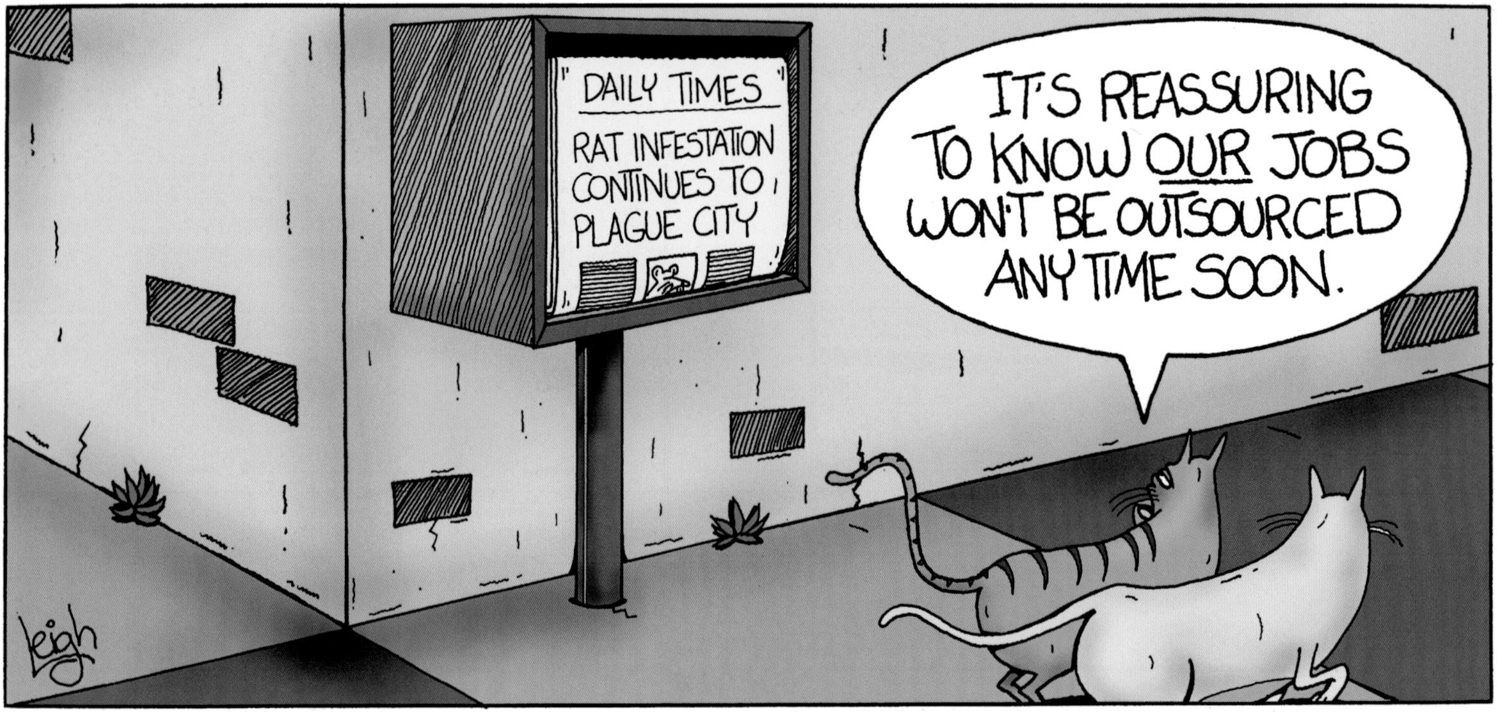
DAILY TIMES
RAT INFESTATION CONTINUES TO PLAGUE CITY
IT'S REASSURING TO KNOW OUR JOBS WON'T BE OUTSOURCED ANY TIME SOON.
Leigh

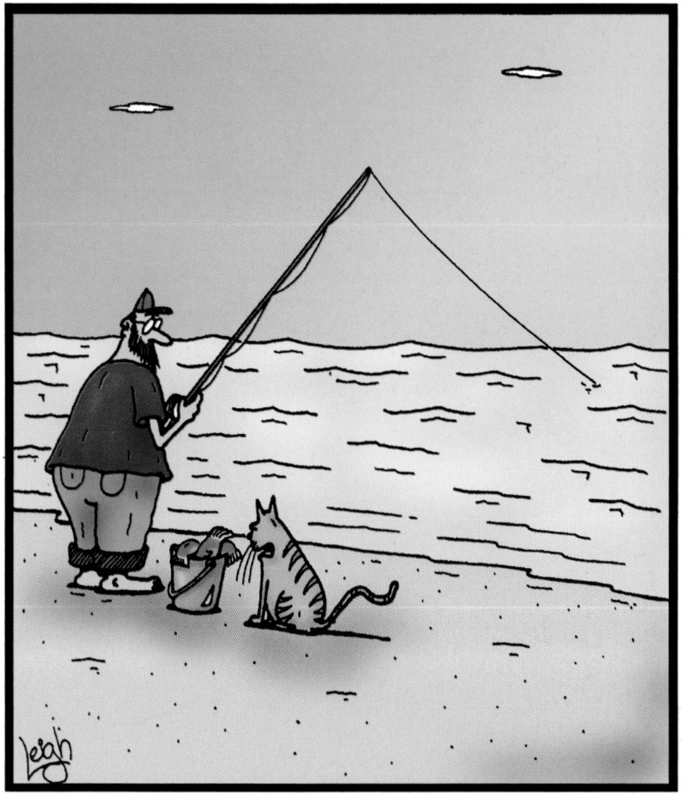

"Consider yourself fortunate, sir, for even though you are quite obviously over the limit, I am in the unique position of sparing you the possible public humiliation and potential legal consequences by simply making your problem go away."

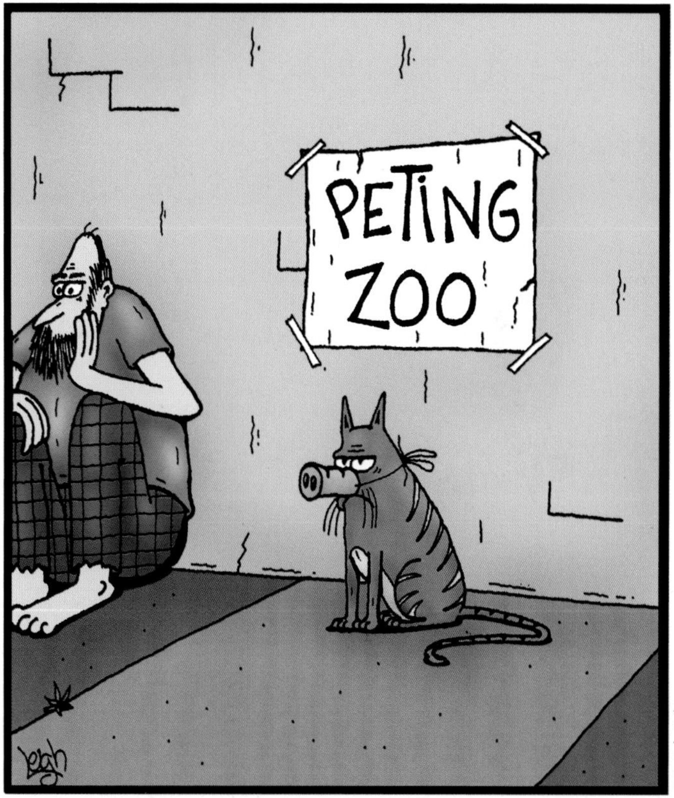
PETING
ZOO

Lloyd starts yet another undercapitalized business venture.

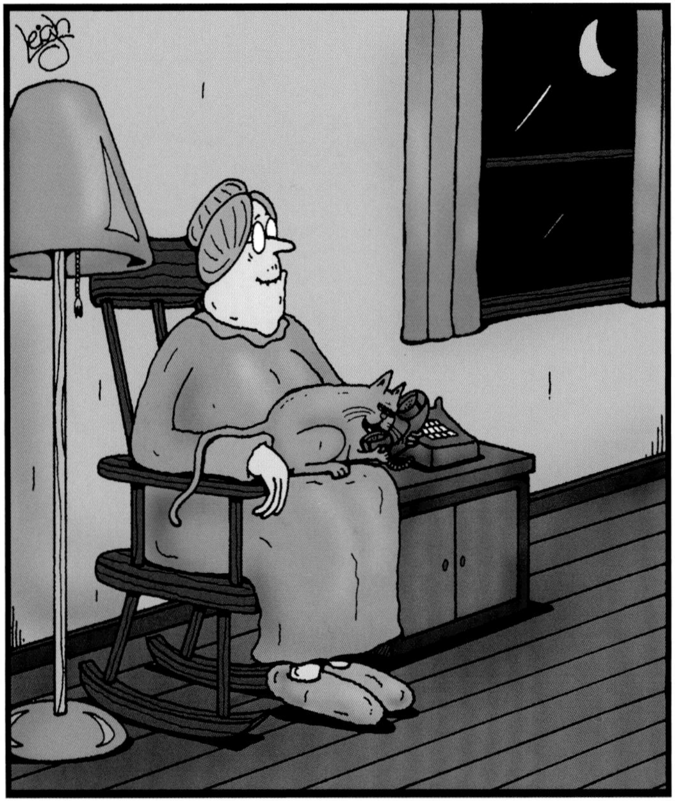
leigh

"Oh, not much ... just rockin' out at home with my ol' lady."

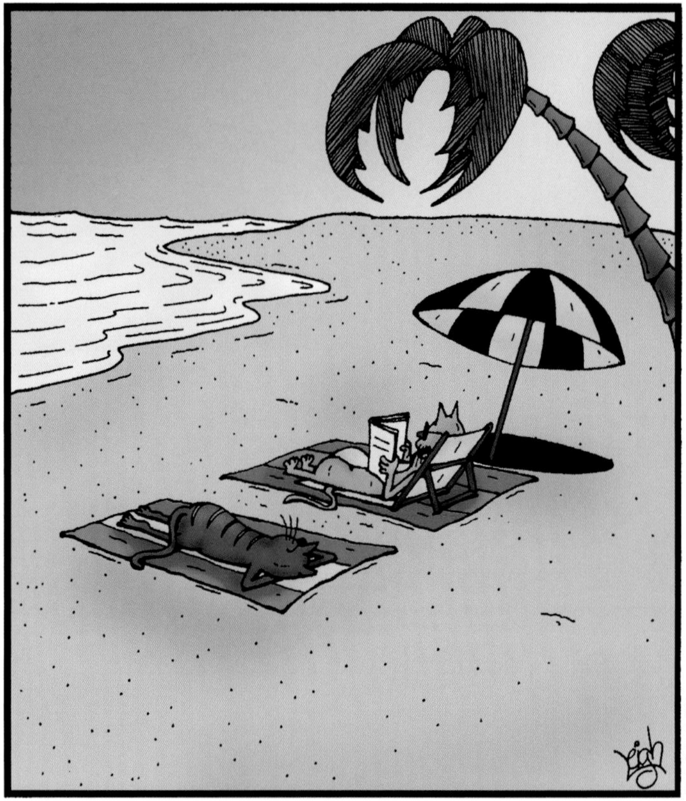
leigh

"... And when the first explorers arrived here, they unwittingly brought rats with them that eventually overrran the entire island. Wow, this place really is a paradise!"

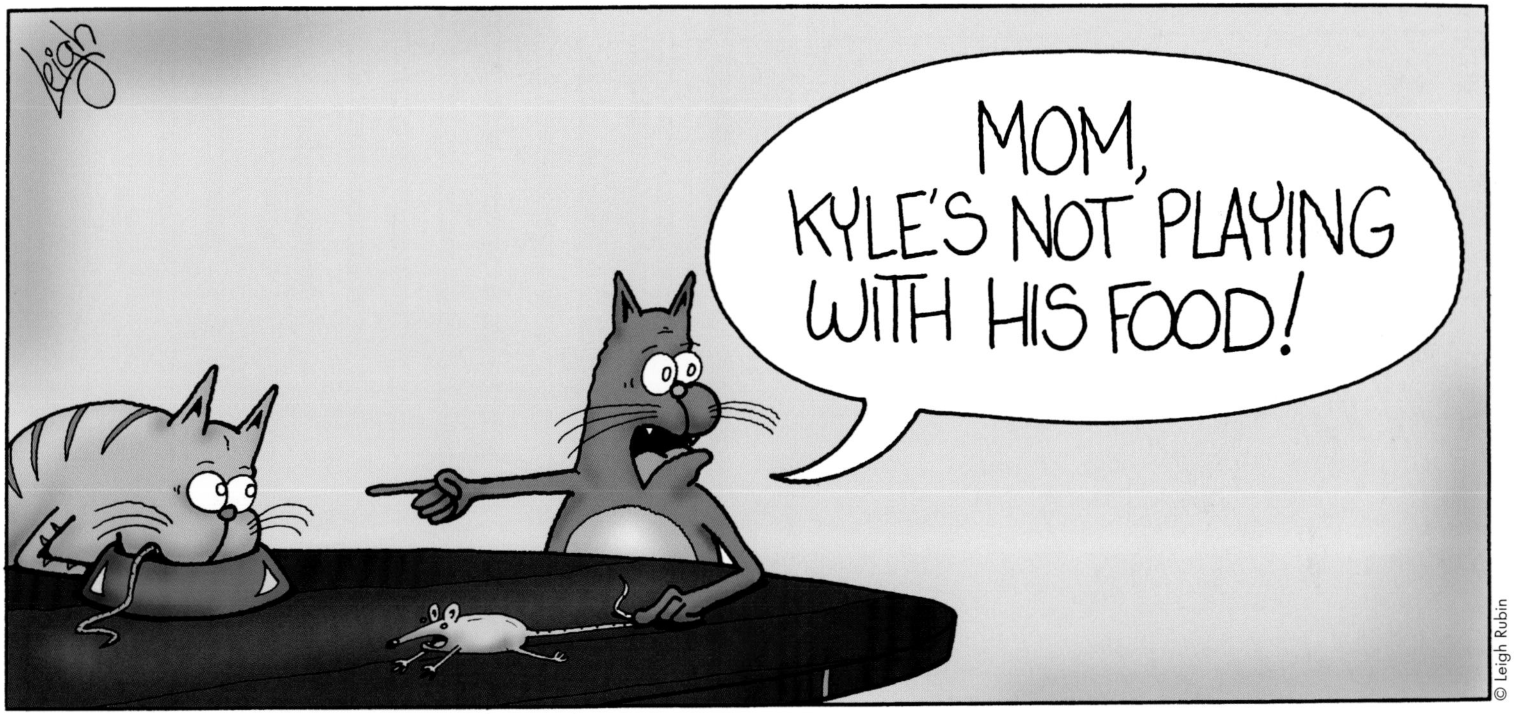
Leigh
MOM, KYLE'S NOT PLAYING WITH HIS FOOD!
© Leigh Rubin

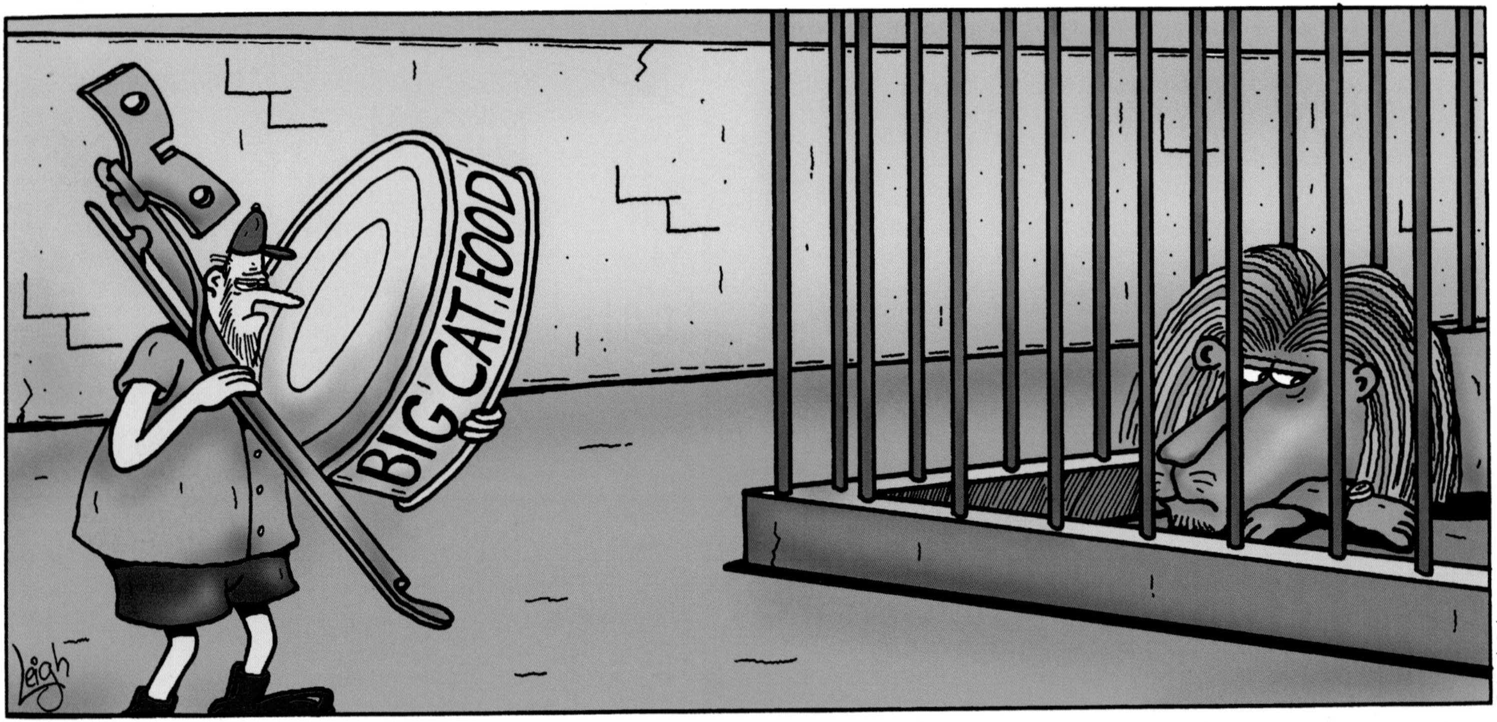
BIG CAT FOOD
Leigh

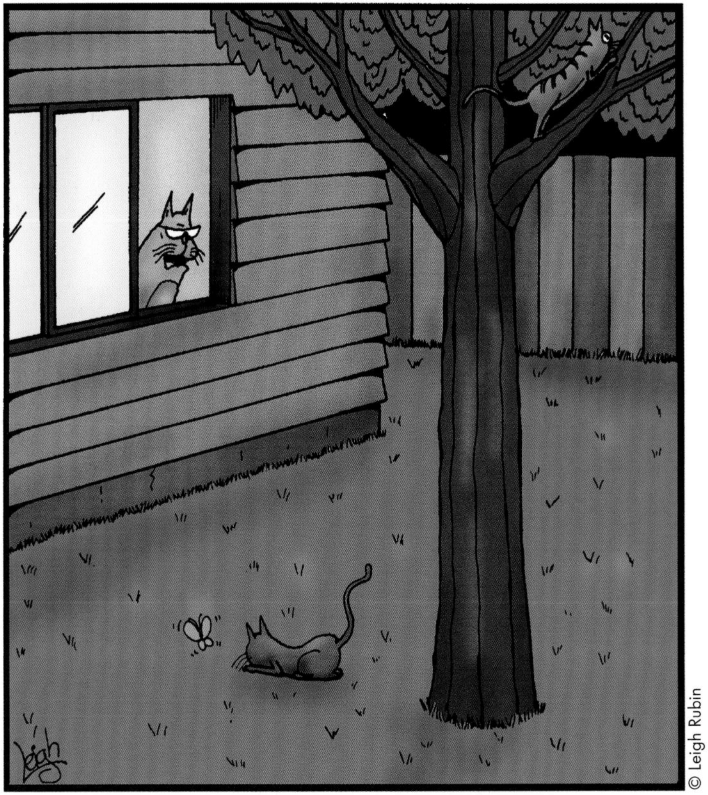
© Leigh Rubin

"Dinner's ready, kids ... Lick your paws, and come to the table!"

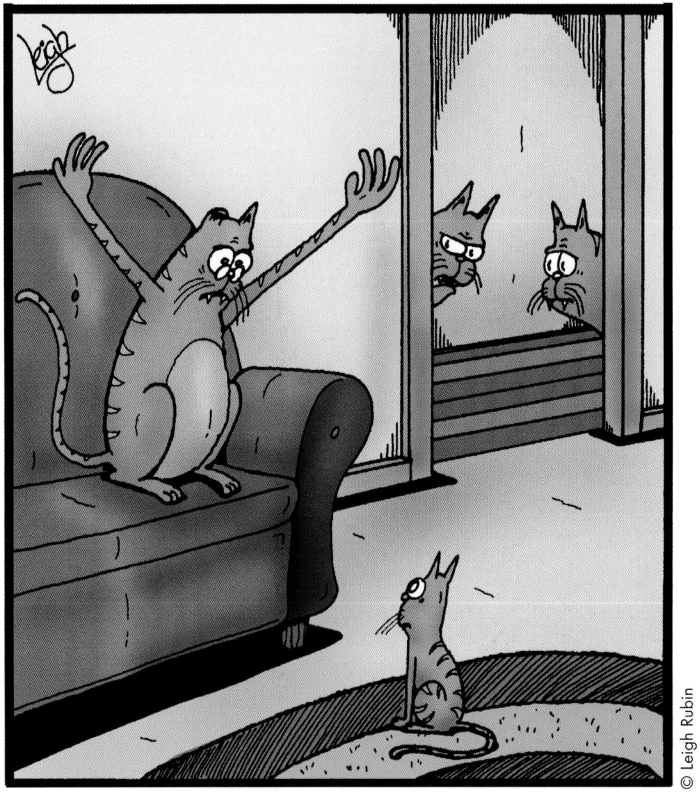
© Leigh Rubin

"... A place called the Magic Kingdom where the mice are as tall as refrigerators?! ... Honestly, George, don't you think it's about time your father lay off the catnip?"

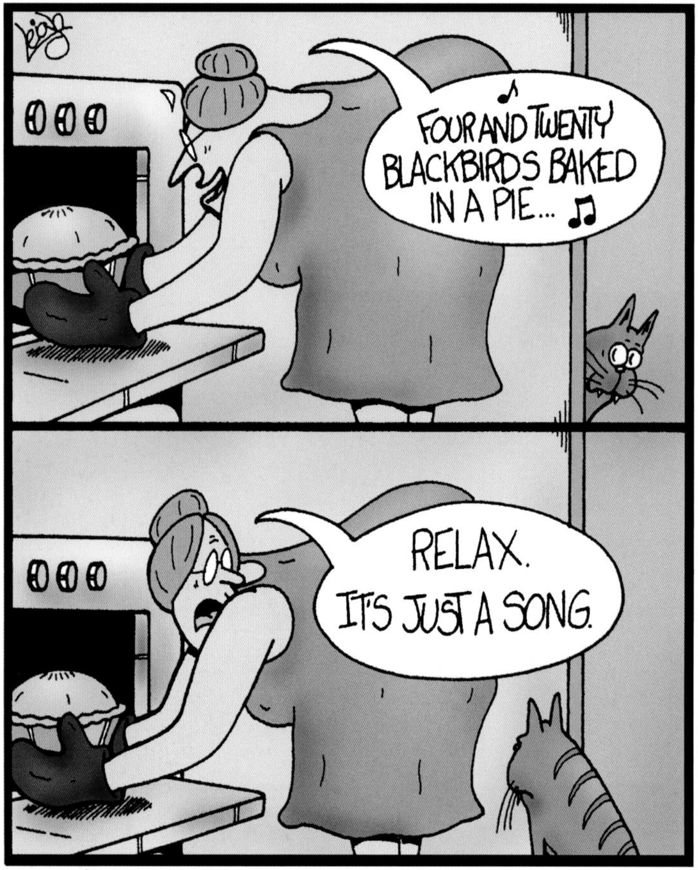
♪ FOUR AND TWENTY BLACKBIRDS BAKED IN A PIE... ♫
RELAX. IT'S JUST A SONG.

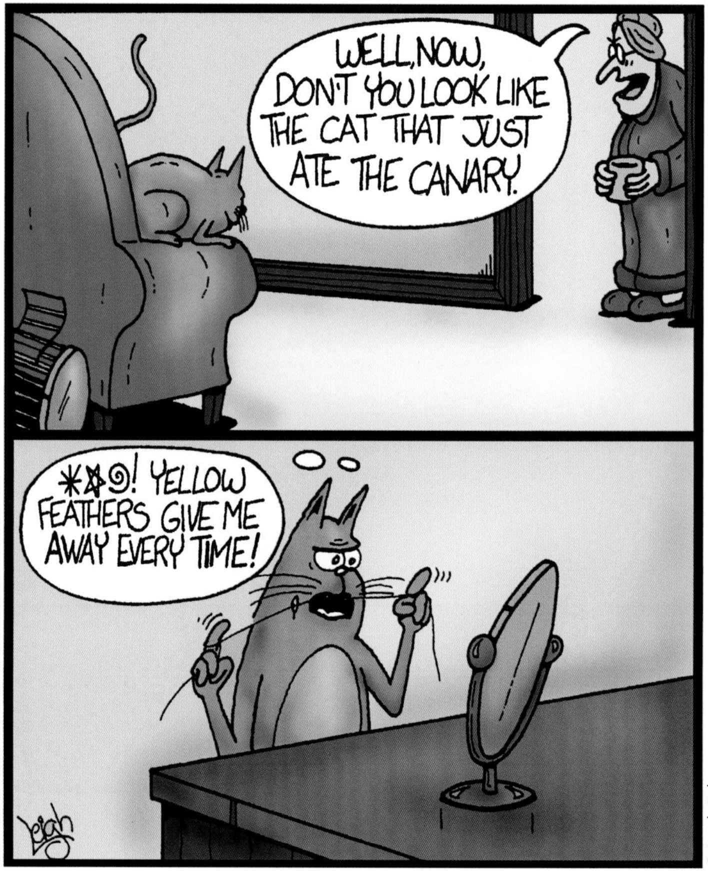
WELL, NOW, DON'T YOU LOOK LIKE THE CAT THAT JUST ATE THE CANARY.
*✡9! YELLOW FEATHERS GIVE ME AWAY EVERY TIME!

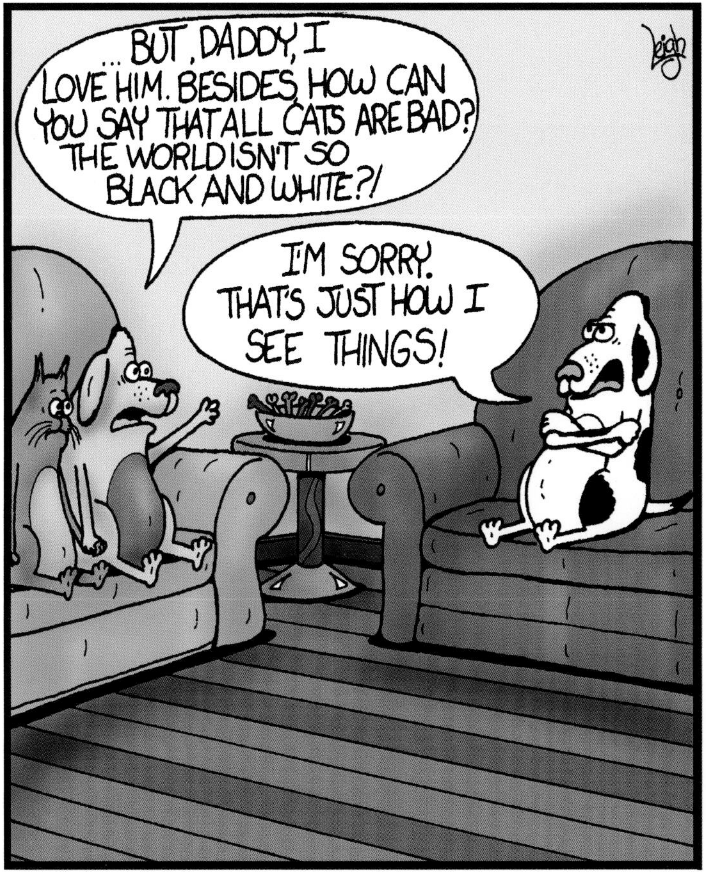
...BUT, DADDY, I LOVE HIM. BESIDES, HOW CAN YOU SAY THAT ALL CATS ARE BAD? THE WORLD ISN'T SO BLACK AND WHITE?!
I'M SORRY. THAT'S JUST HOW I SEE THINGS!
Leigh

© Leigh Rubin

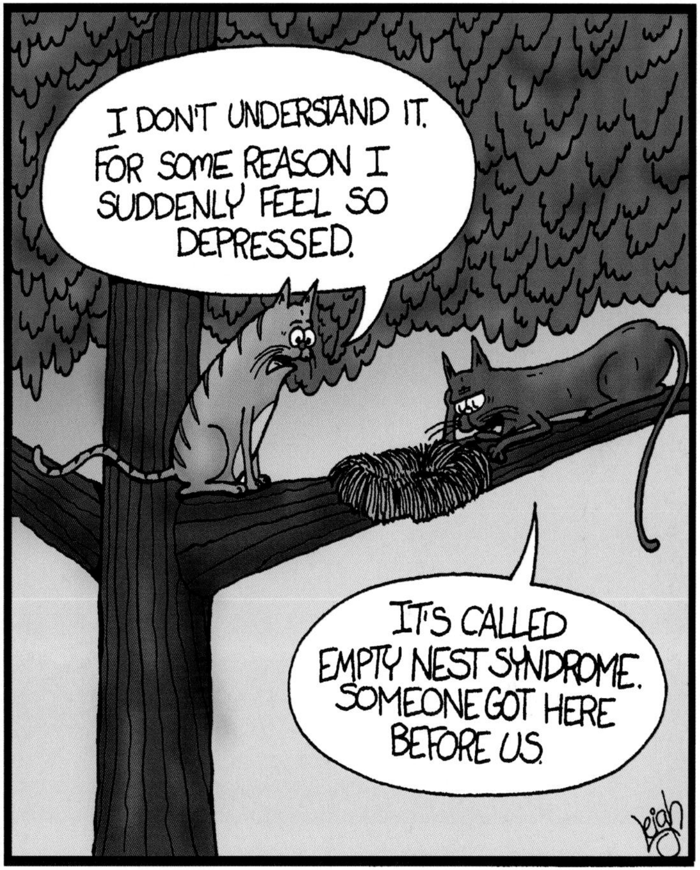
I DON'T UNDERSTAND IT. FOR SOME REASON I SUDDENLY FEEL SO DEPRESSED.
IT'S CALLED EMPTY NEST SYNDROME. SOMEONE GOT HERE BEFORE US.
Leigh

© Leigh Rubin

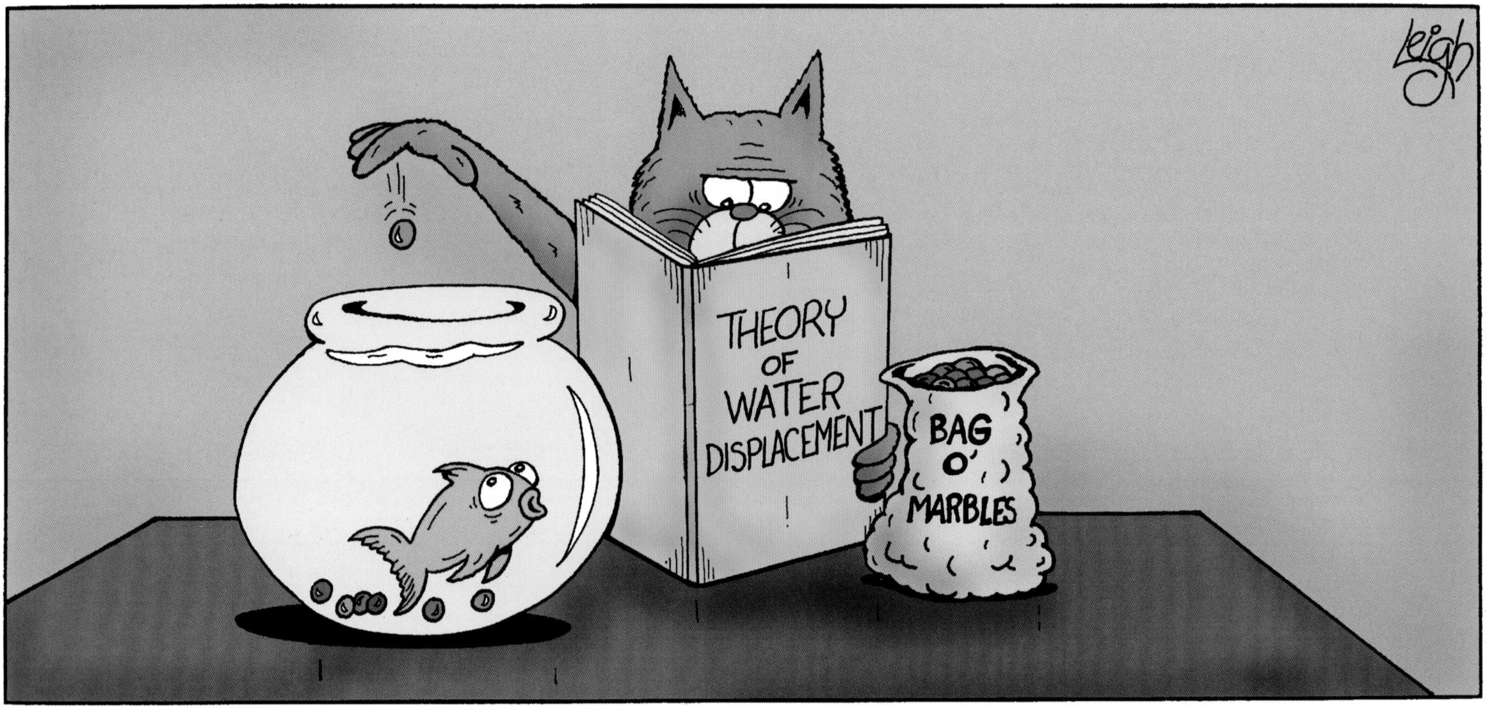
Leigh
THEORY OF WATER DISPLACEMENT
BAG O' MARBLES

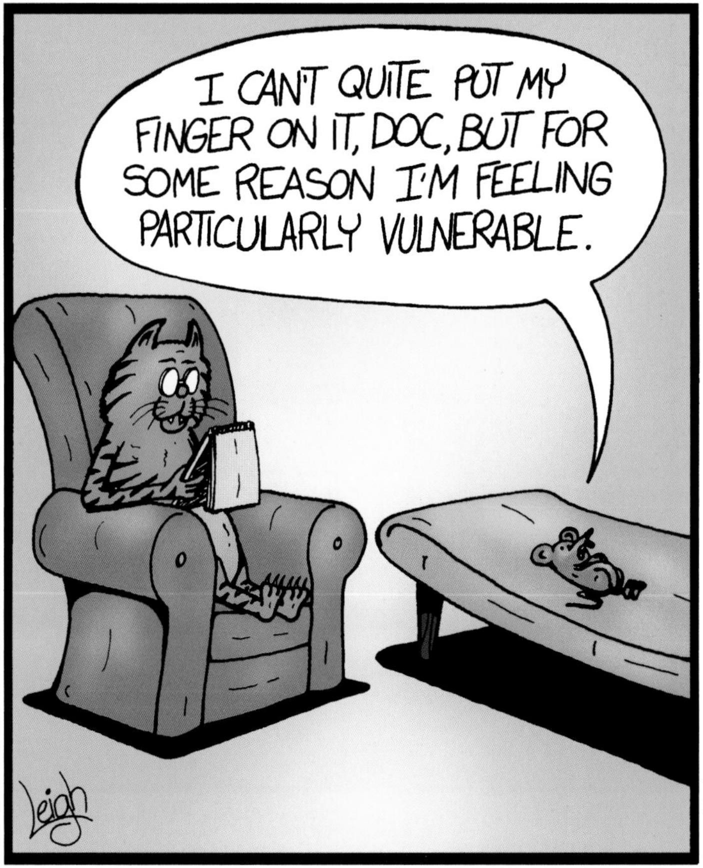
I CAN'T QUITE PUT MY FINGER ON IT, DOC, BUT FOR SOME REASON I'M FEELING PARTICULARLY VULNERABLE.
Leigh

© Leigh Rubin

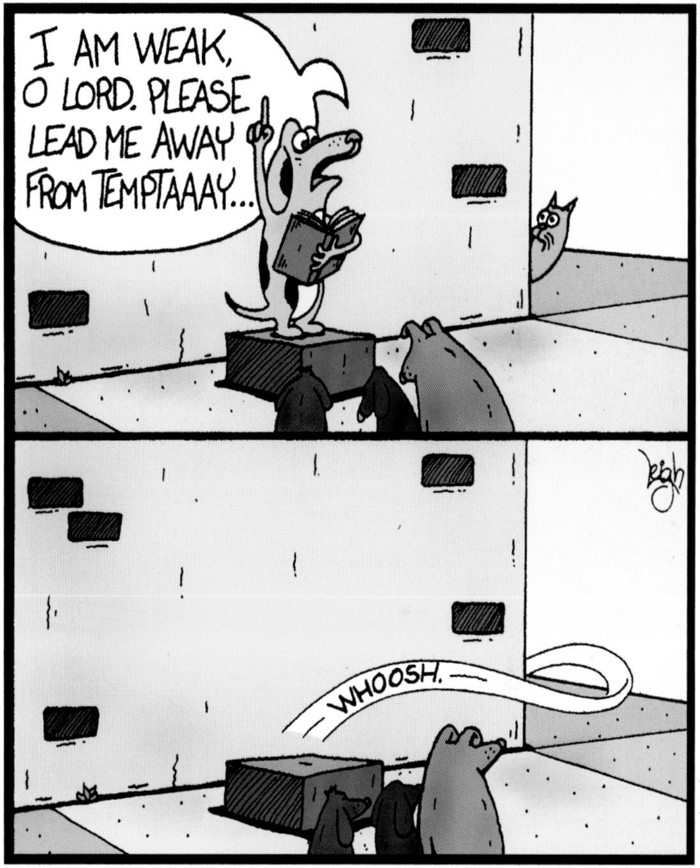
I AM WEAK, O LORD. PLEASE LEAD ME AWAY FROM TEMPTAAAY...
Leigh
WHOOSH

© Leigh Rubin

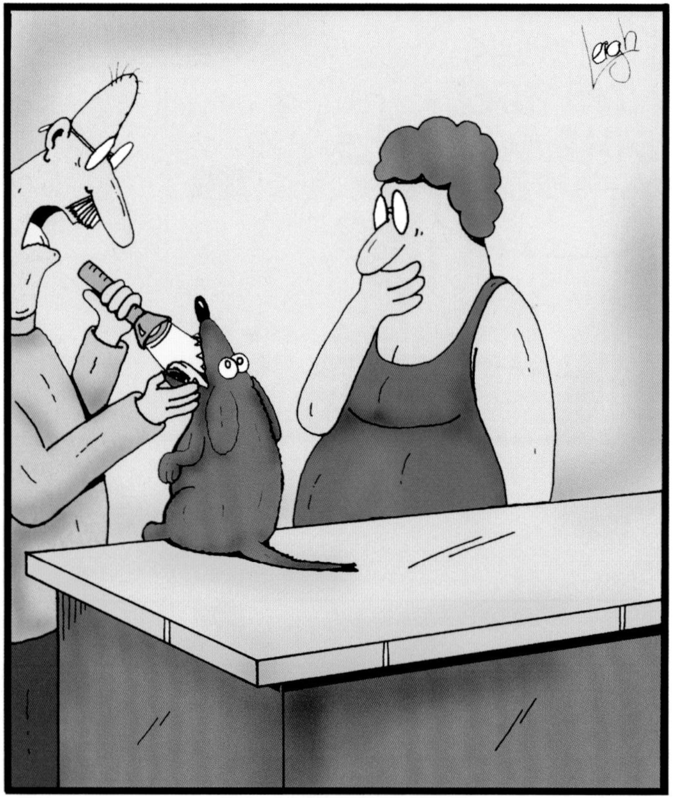
leigh

"Nope ... no sign of your kitten, Ma'am. But to be absolutely certain, we'd better perform a CAT scan."

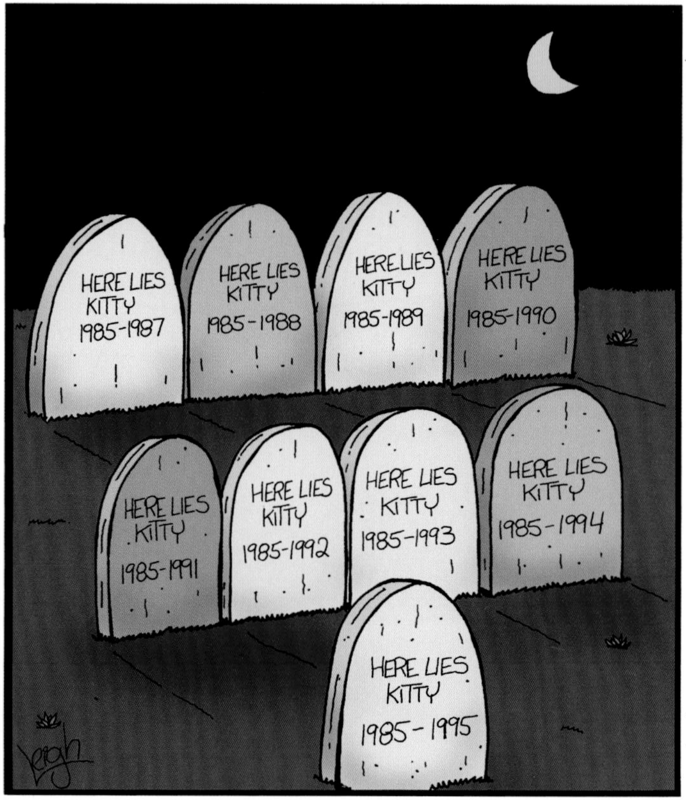
HERE LIES KITTY 1985-1987
HERE LIES KITTY 1985-1988
HERE LIES KITTY 1985-1989
HERE LIES KITTY 1985-1990
HERE LIES KITTY 1985-1991
HERE LIES KITTY 1985-1992
HERE LIES KITTY 1985-1993
HERE LIES KITTY 1985-1994
HERE LIES KITTY 1985-1995
leigh

Cat burial plots

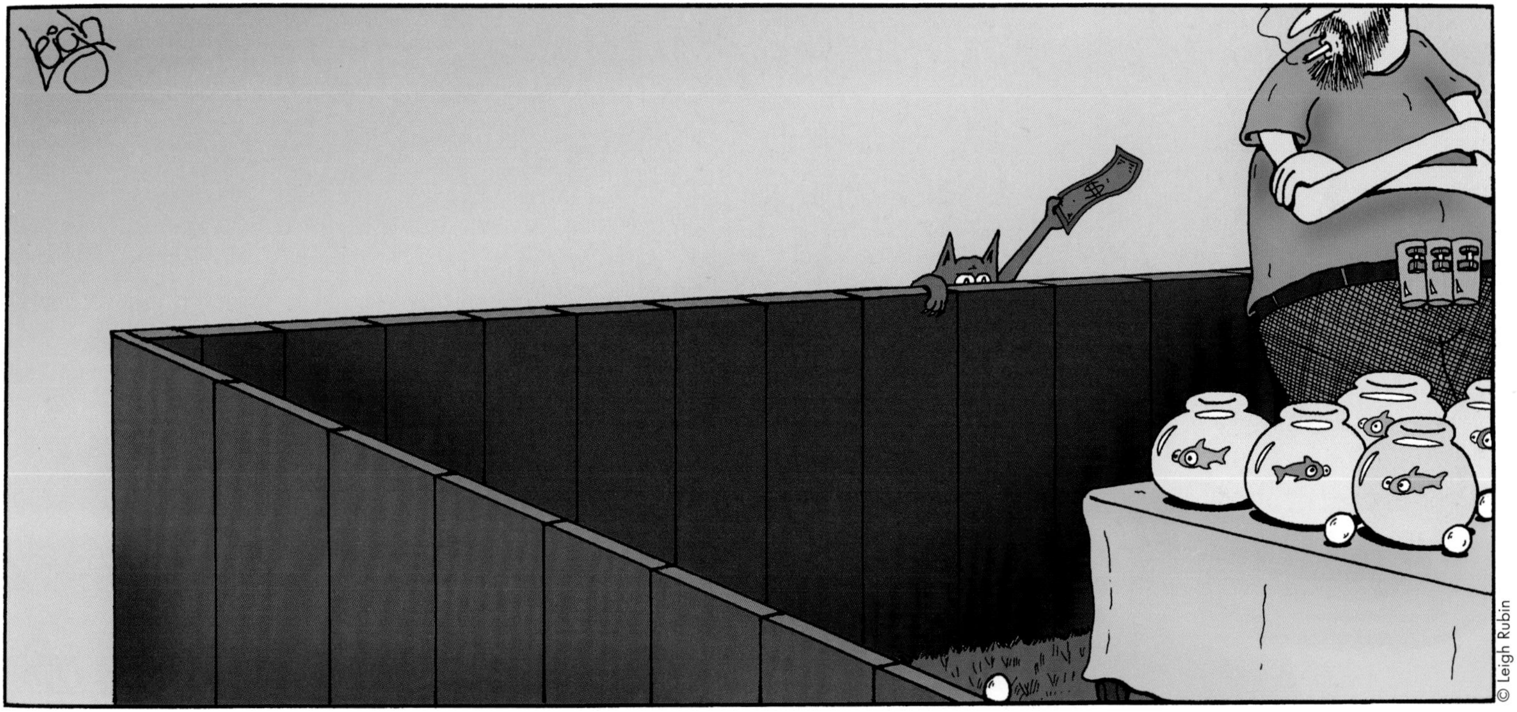
leigh
© Leigh Rubin

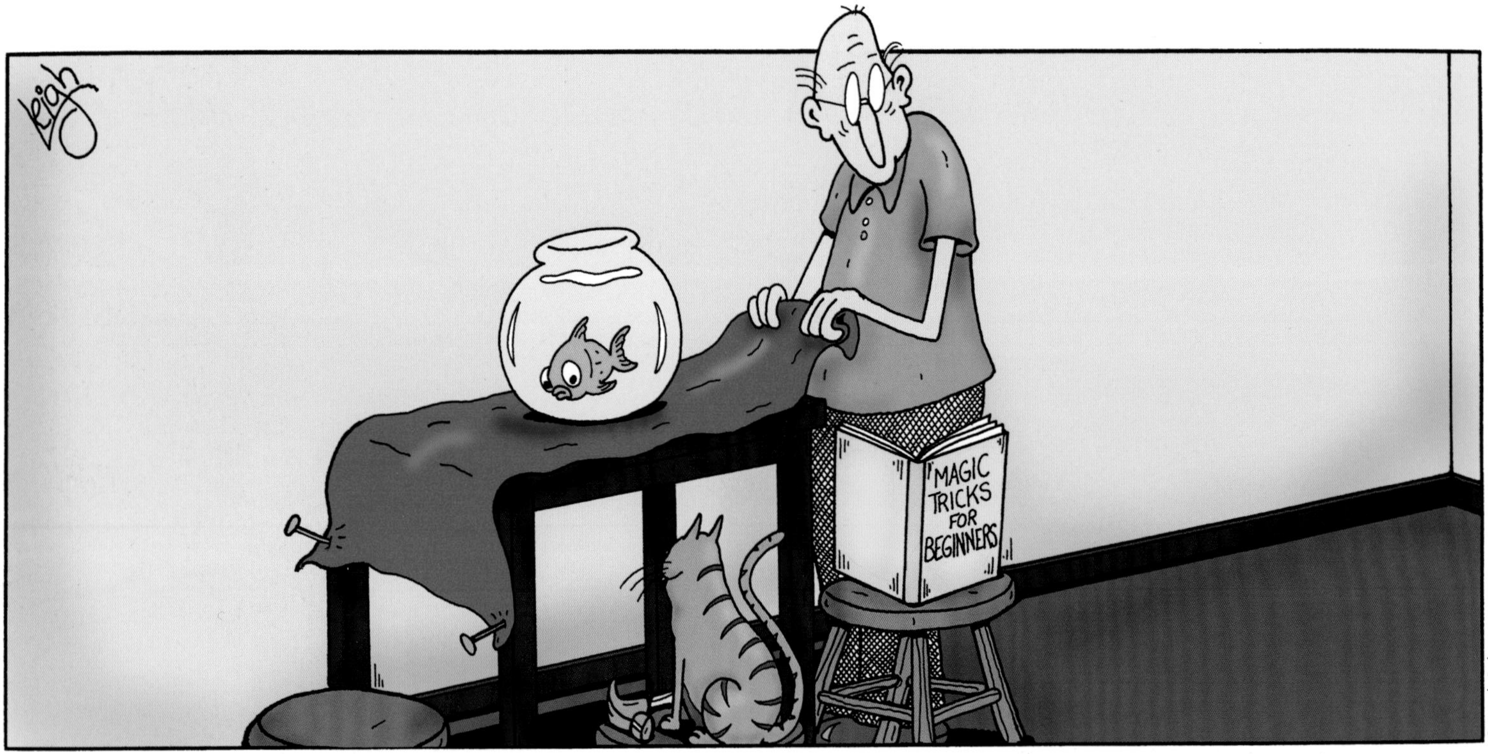

MAGIC TRICKS FOR BEGINNERS

© Leigh Rubin

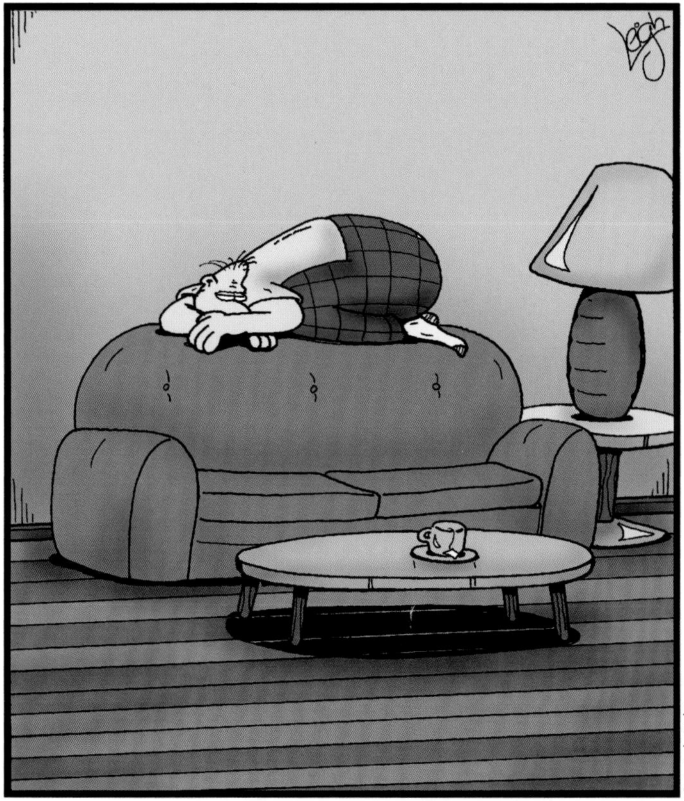
Leigh

Every afternoon, Herb enjoyed
a nice, relaxing catnap.

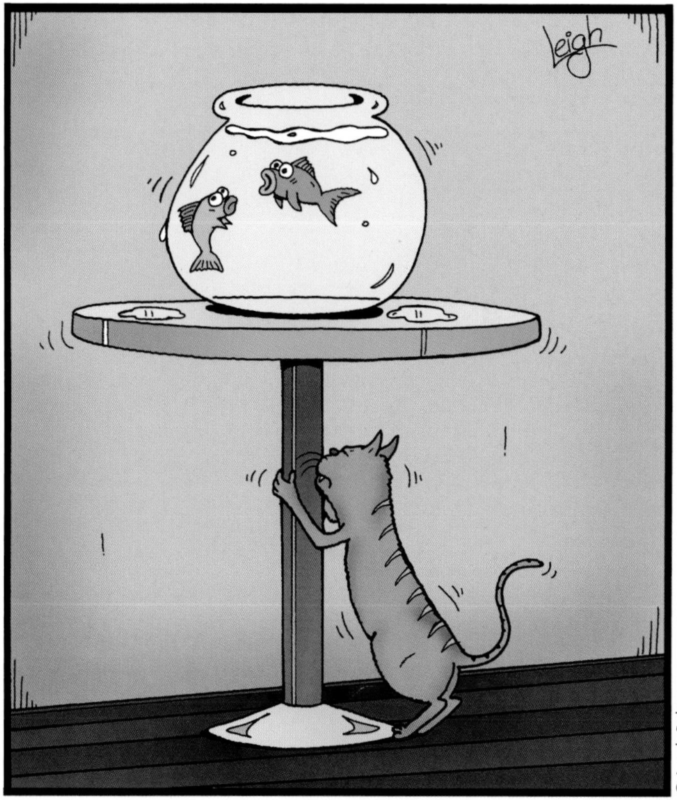
Leigh

"Whoa, that was some earthquake! ...
Un oh, you'd better hold on. I feel
another one coming!"

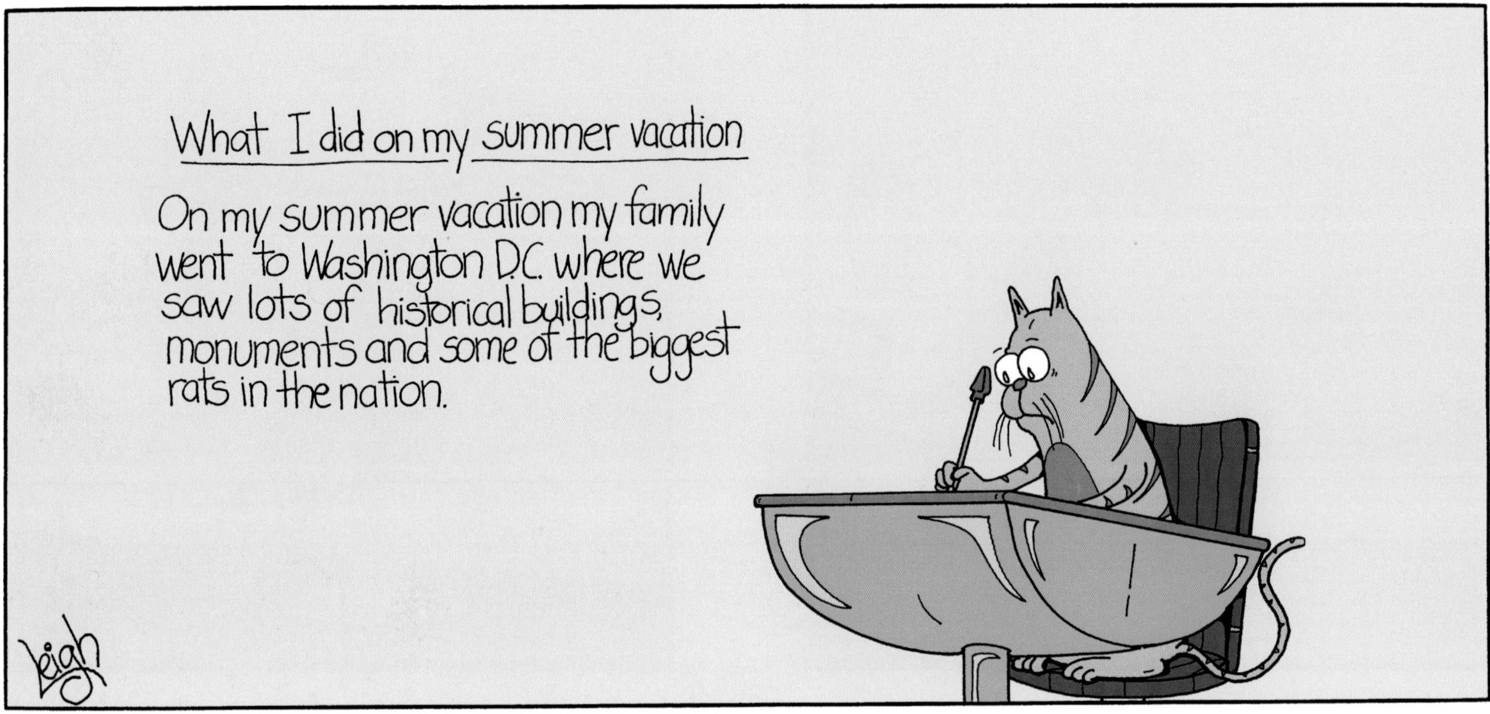
What I did on my summer vacation
On my summer vacation my family went to Washington D.C. where we saw lots of historical buildings, monuments and some of the biggest rats in the nation.
leigh

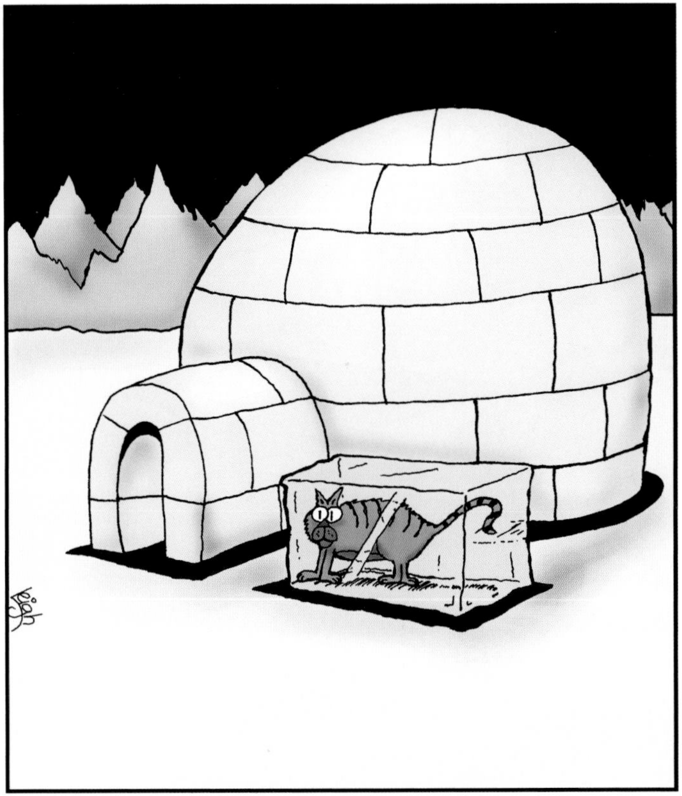

Six months had passed since
Nanook had put the cat out for the night.

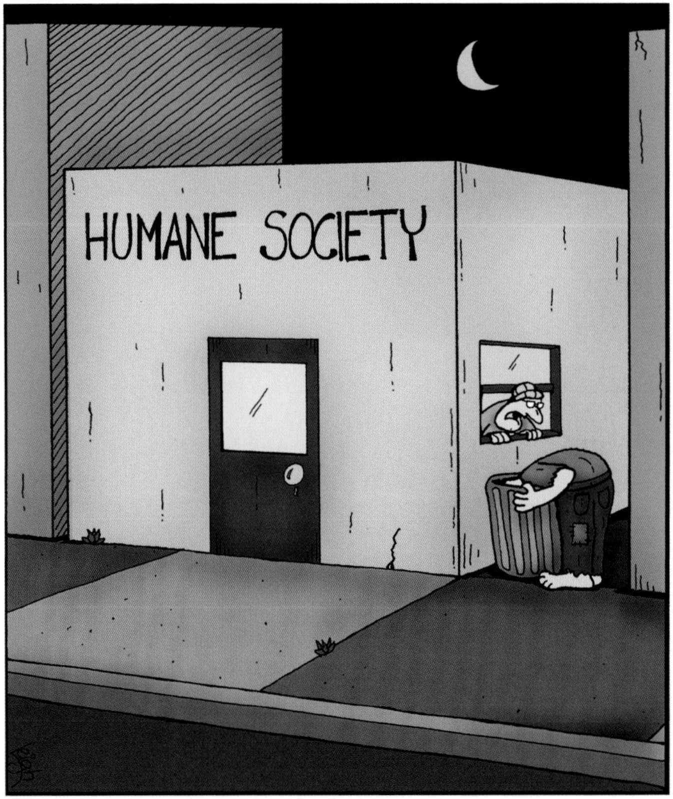
HUMANE SOCIETY

"Hey there... you leave that for the cats!"

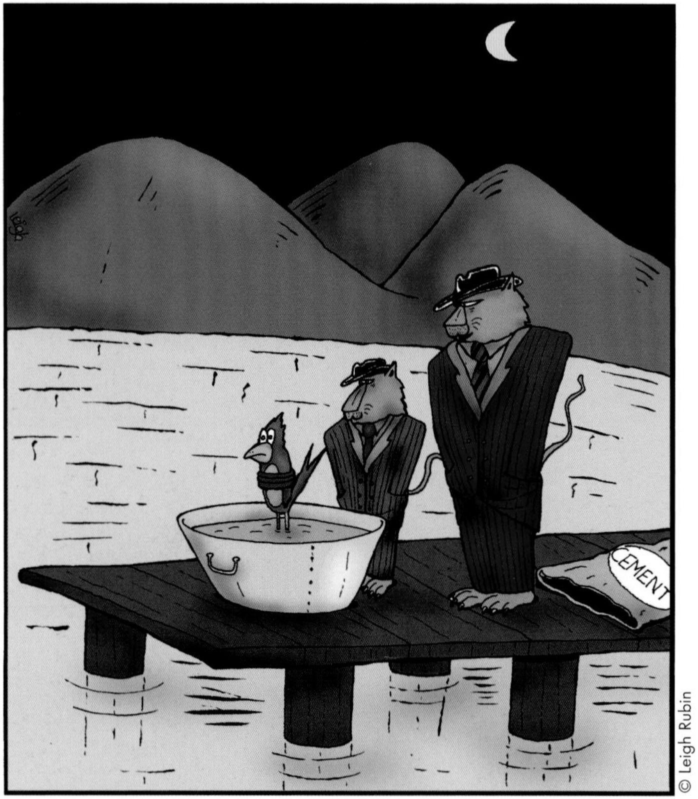

CEMENT
© Leigh Rubin

"A little boidy told me! A little boidy told me! Well a little boidy won't be tellin' nuthin' to nobody no more!"

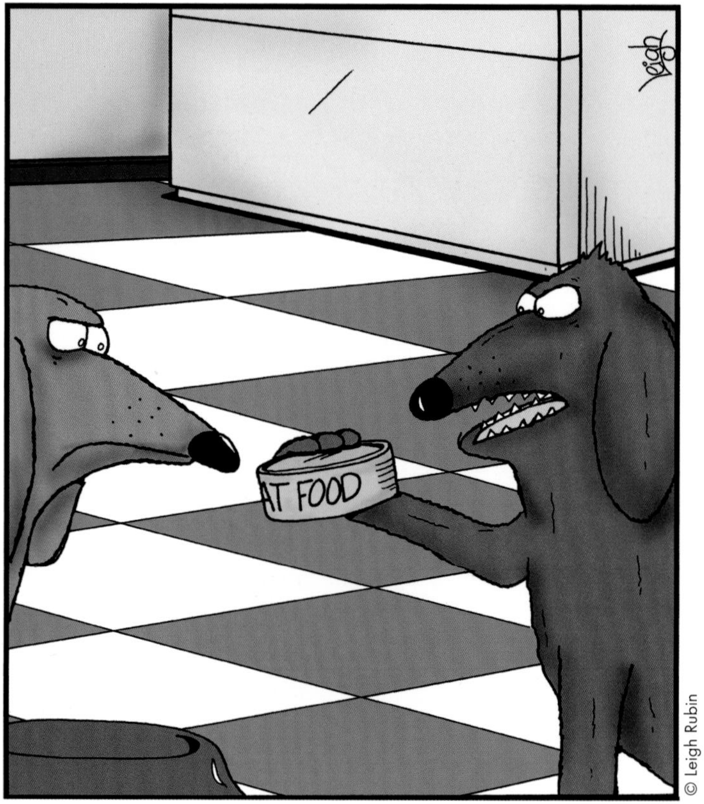

AT FOOD
© Leigh Rubin

"What a rip off! Where do they come off calling this stuff cat food? Just look at the ingredients... there's not any cat in it!"

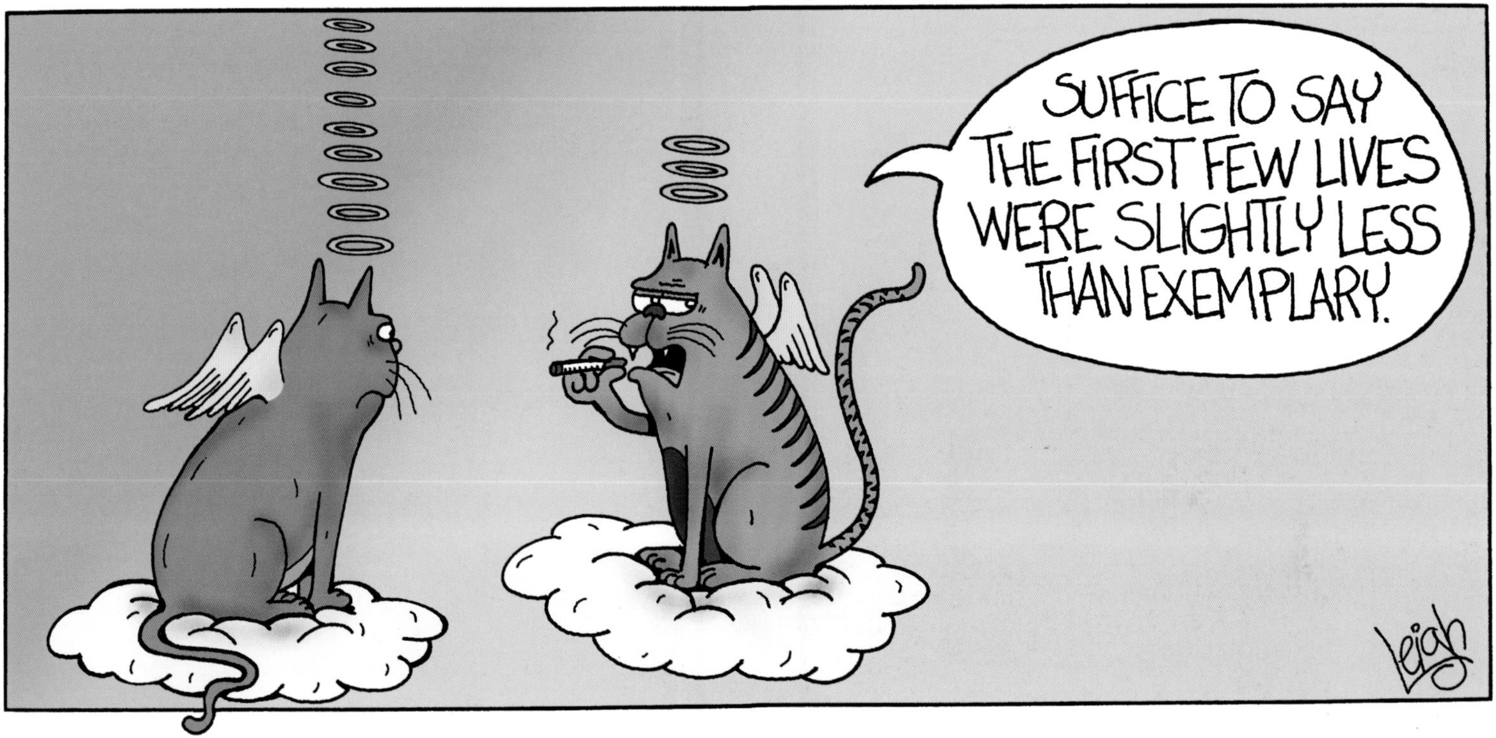
SUFFICE TO SAY THE FIRST FEW LIVES WERE SLIGHTLY LESS THAN EXEMPLARY.
Leigh

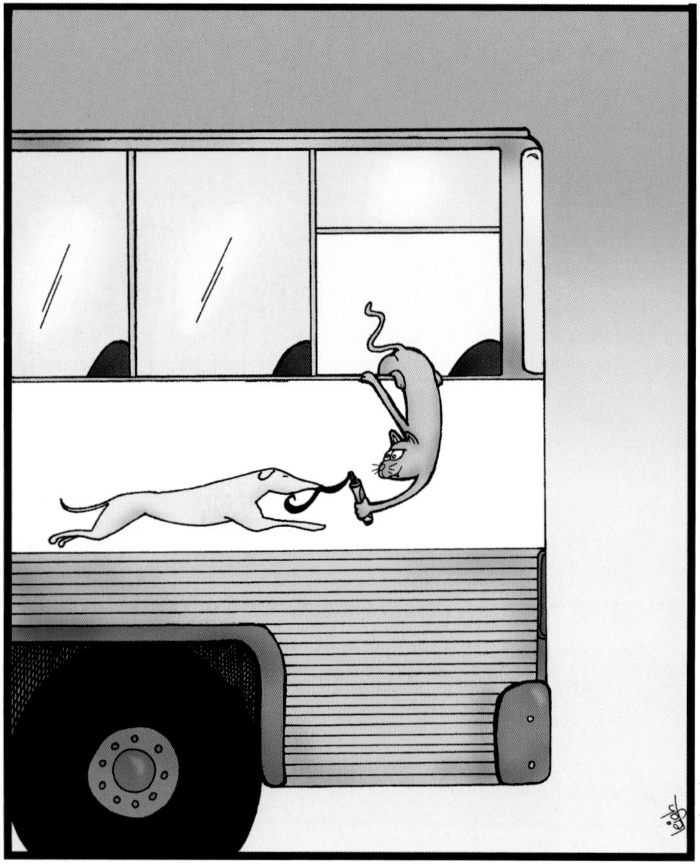
leigh

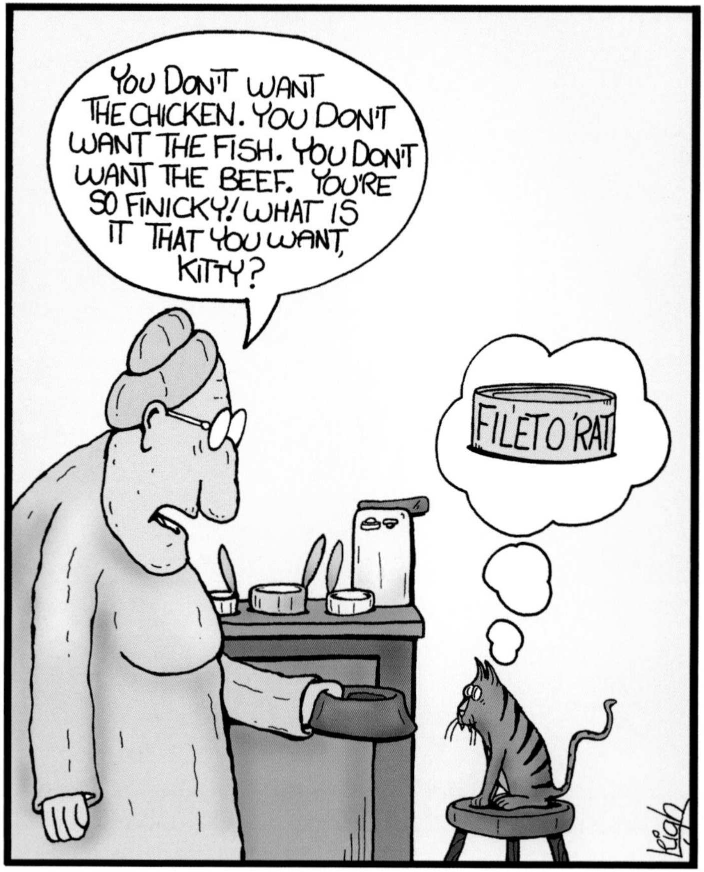
YOU DON'T WANT THE CHICKEN. YOU DON'T WANT THE FISH. YOU DON'T WANT THE BEEF. YOU'RE SO FINICKY! WHAT IS IT THAT YOU WANT, KITTY?
FILET O'RAT
leigh

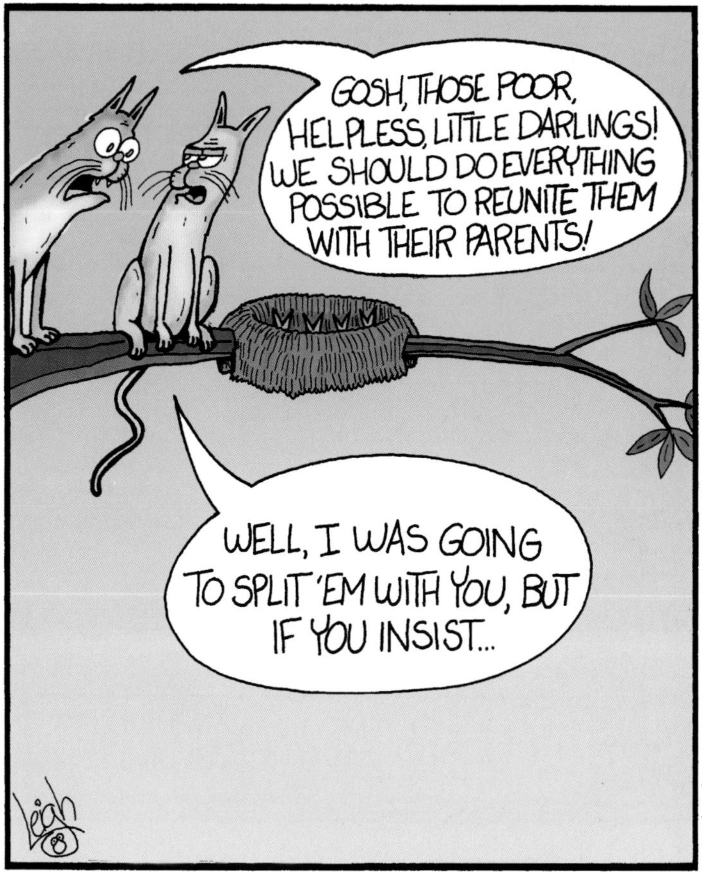
GOSH, THOSE POOR, HELPLESS, LITTLE DARLINGS! WE SHOULD DO EVERYTHING POSSIBLE TO REUNITE THEM WITH THEIR PARENTS!
WELL, I WAS GOING TO SPLIT 'EM WITH YOU, BUT IF YOU INSIST...

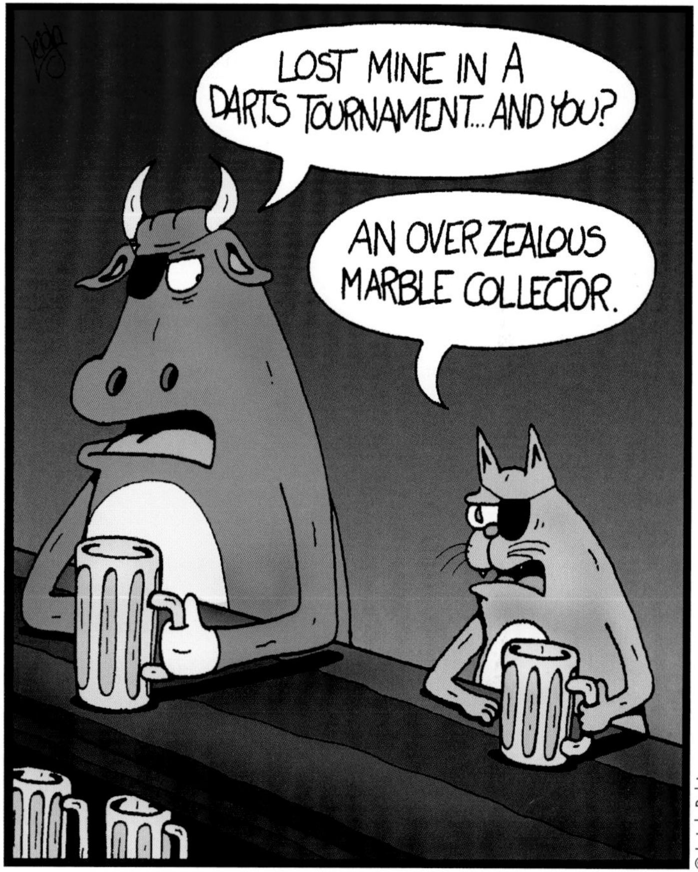
LOST MINE IN A DARTS TOURNAMENT... AND YOU?
AN OVERZEALOUS MARBLE COLLECTOR.

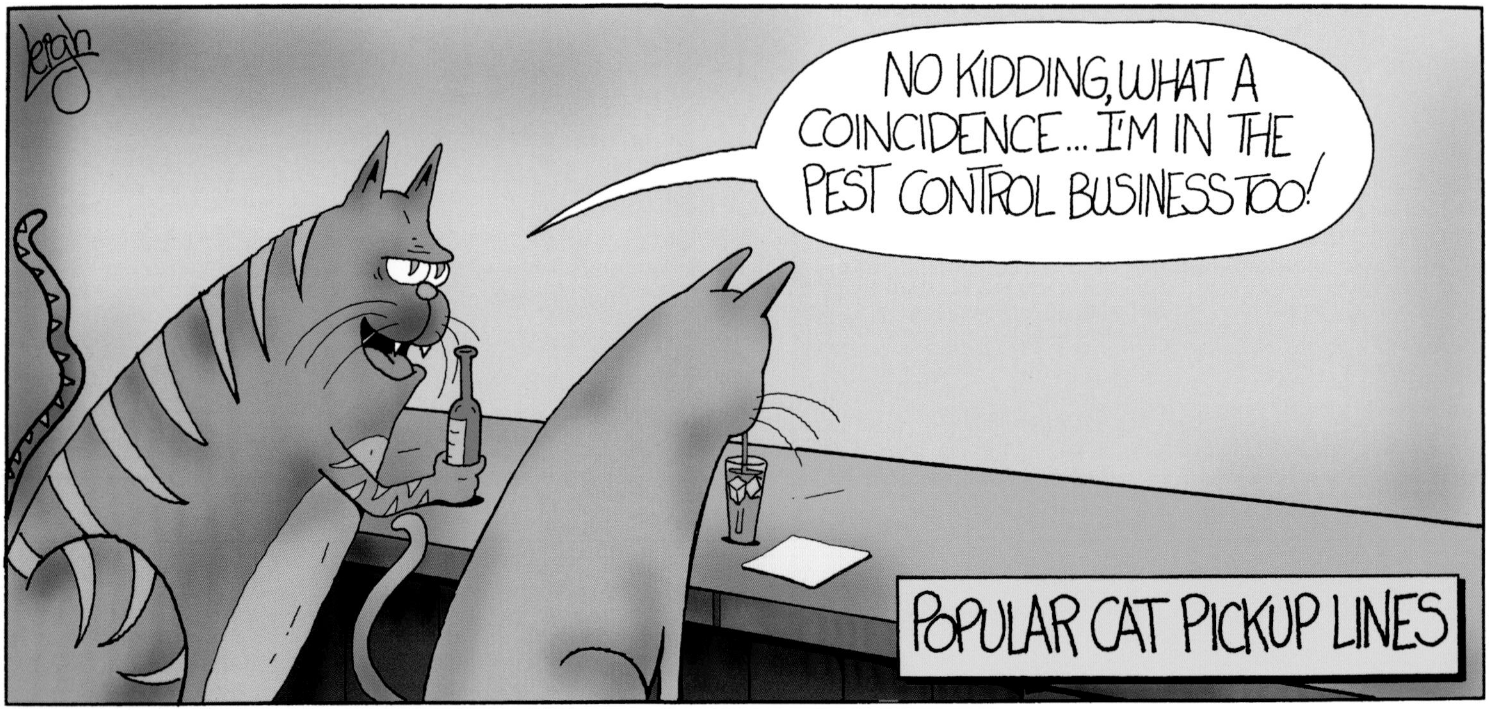
Leigh
NO KIDDING, WHAT A COINCIDENCE... I'M IN THE PEST CONTROL BUSINESS TOO!
POPULAR CAT PICKUP LINES

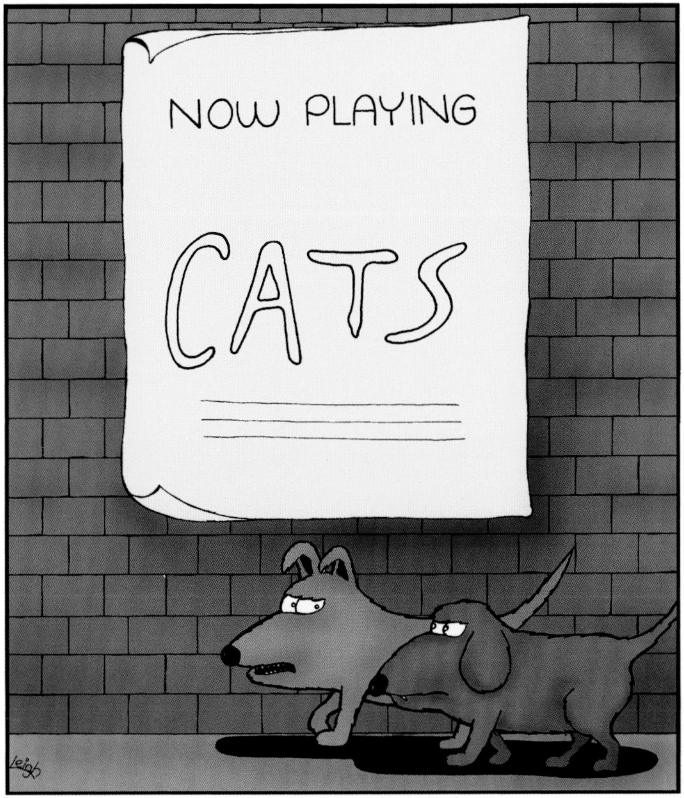
NOW PLAYING
CATS
leigh

"I thought it was lousy."

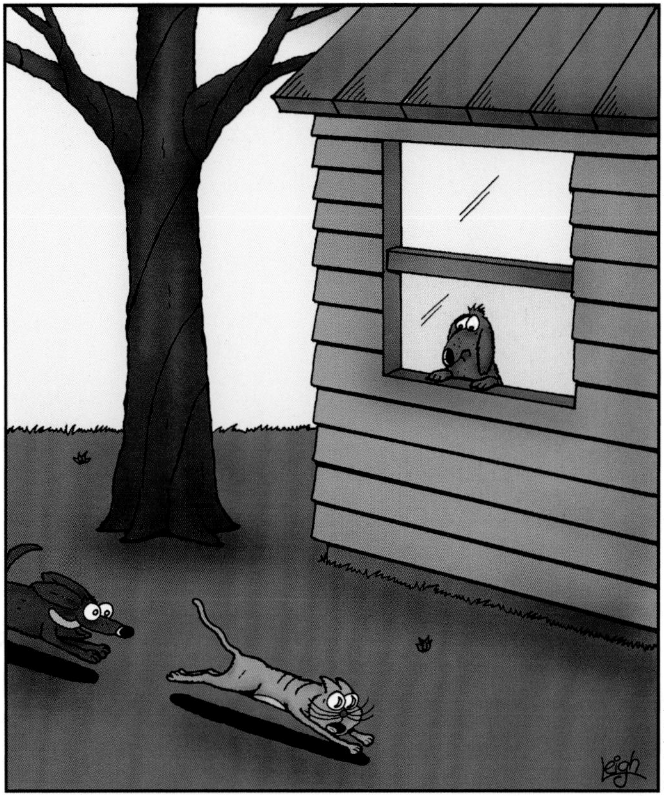
Leigh

Ralph wished he could go out and have fun like the other dogs but unfortunately he was allergic to cats.

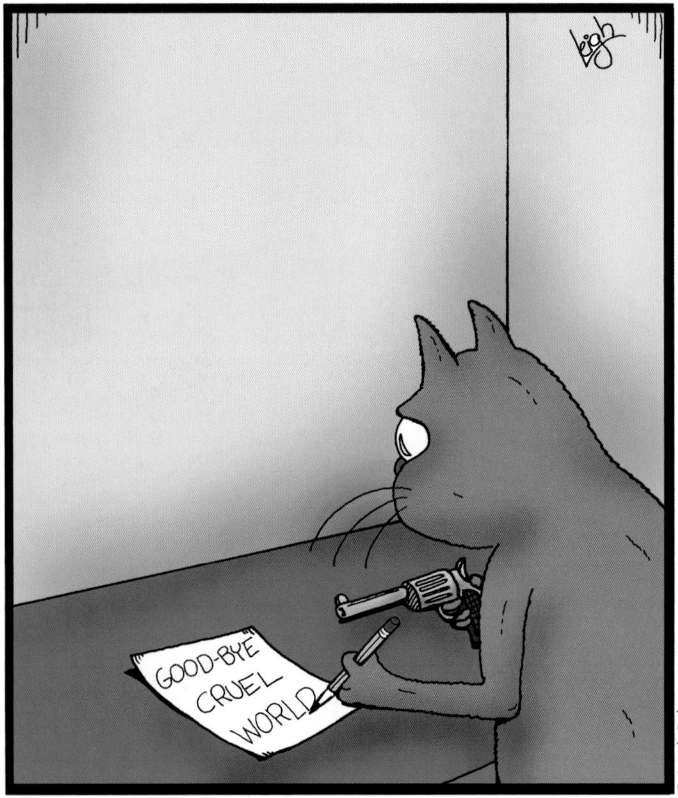
leigh
GOOD-BYE
CRUEL
WORLD

Fluffy's desperate attempt to end it all failed as he only had eight bullets.

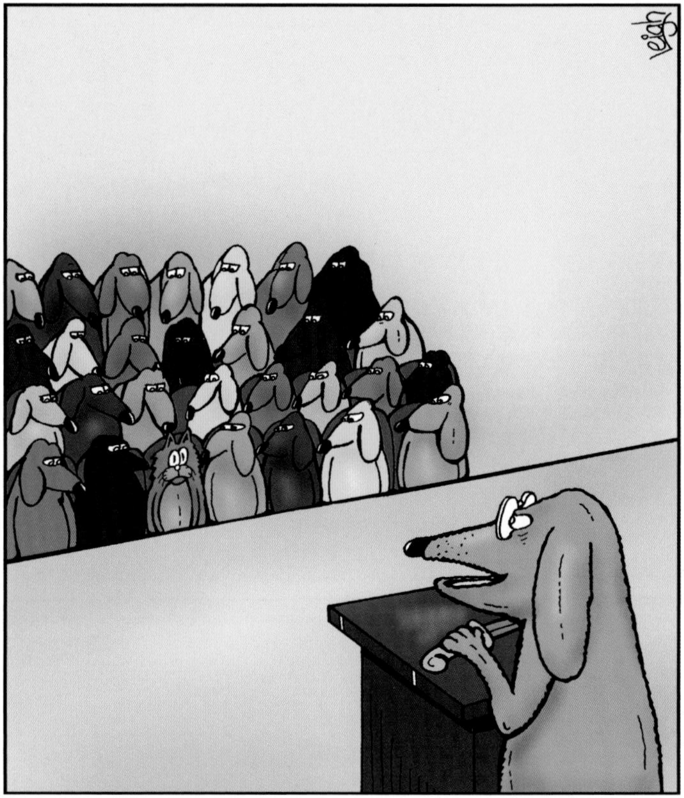
leigh

"In order to adequately demonstrate just how many ways there are to skin a cat, I'll need a volunteer from the audience."

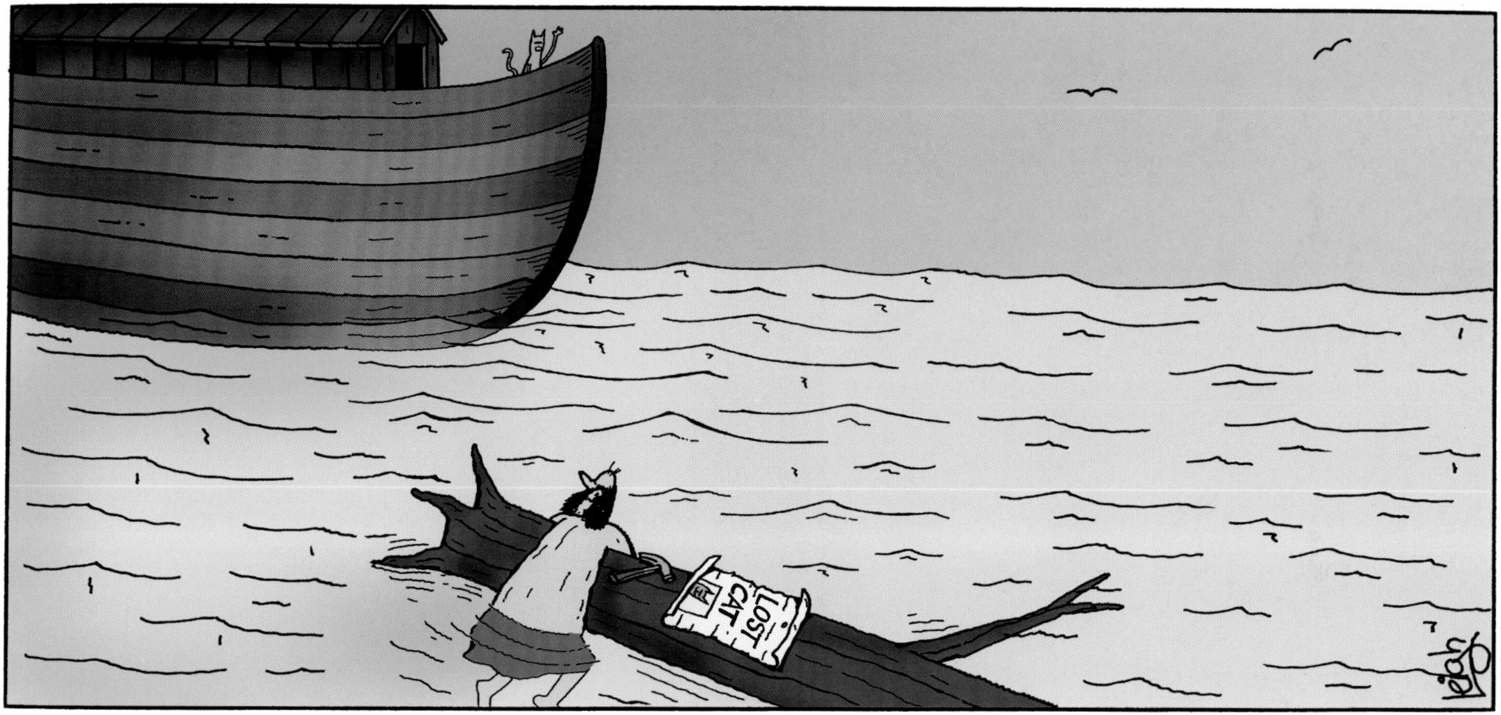
LOST
CAT

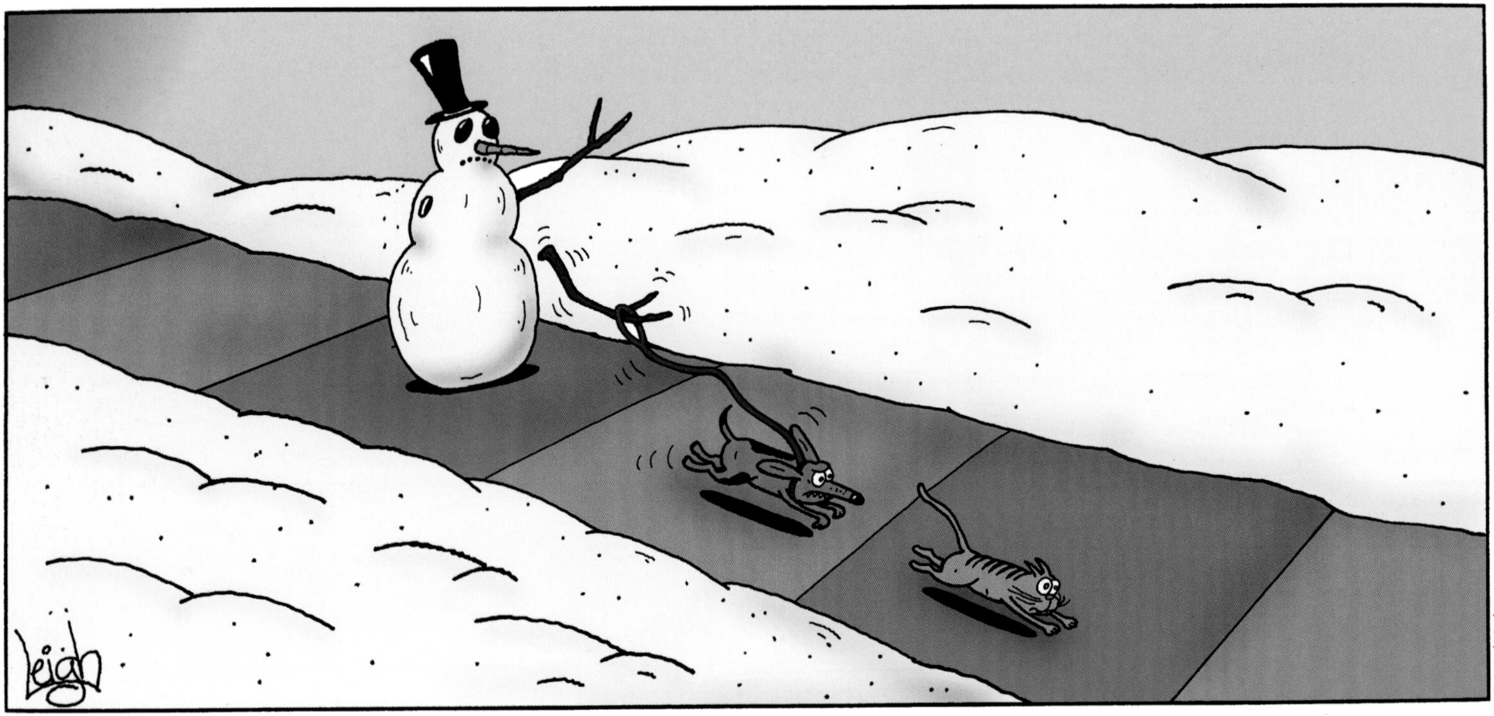
Leigh

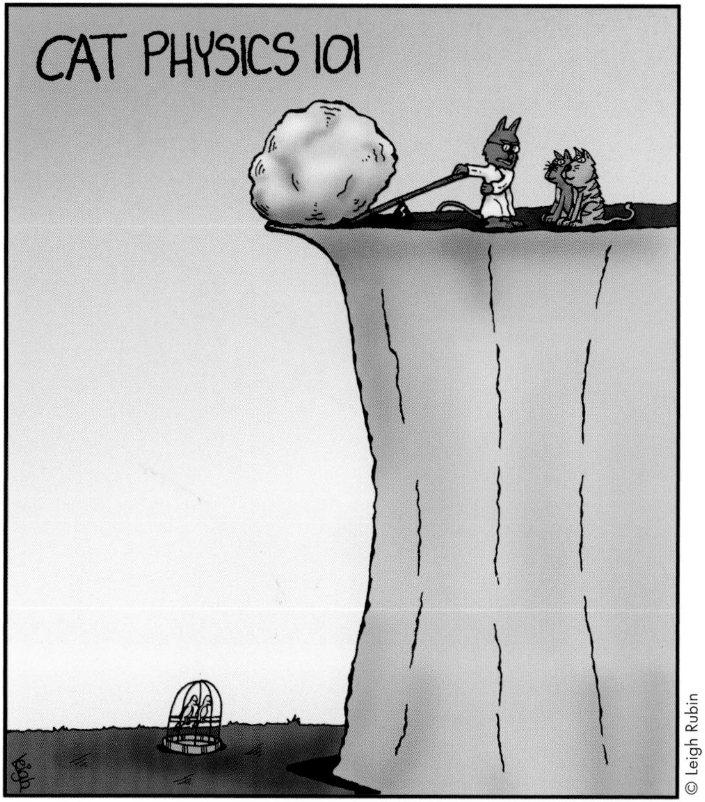
CAT PHYSICS 101
leigh
© Leigh Rubin

"Now, observe carefully as I demonstrate the 'two birds, one stone' theory."

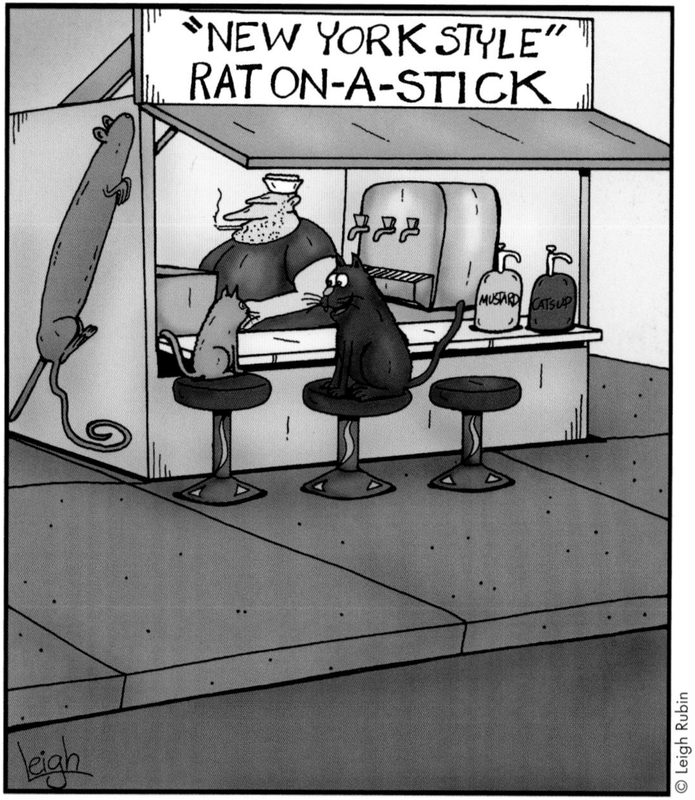
"NEW YORK STYLE" RAT ON-A-STICK
MUSTARD
CATSUP
leigh
© Leigh Rubin

"I love this place. It's just like they used to make 'em back in Brooklyn. Three feet long."

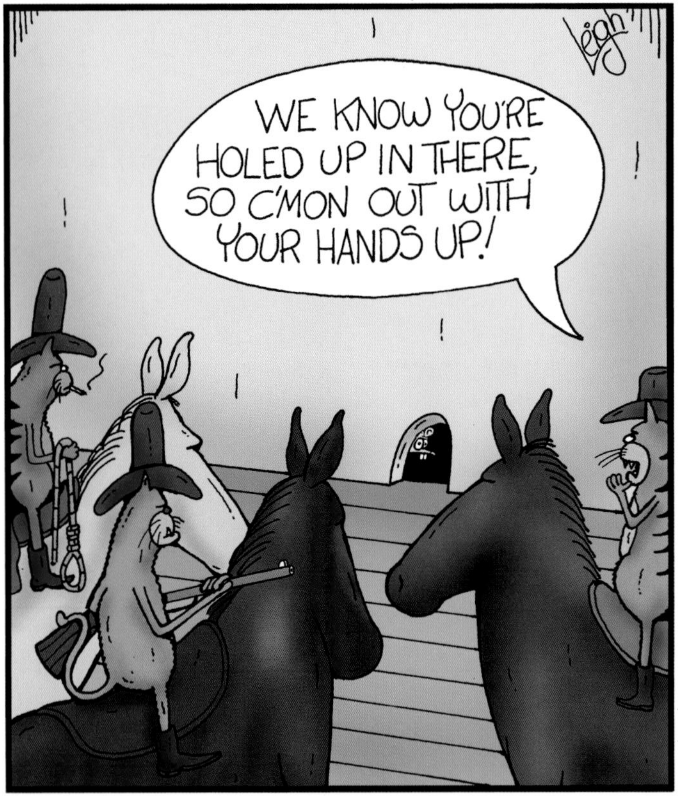
WE KNOW YOU'RE HOLED UP IN THERE, SO C'MON OUT WITH YOUR HANDS UP!

Posse cats.

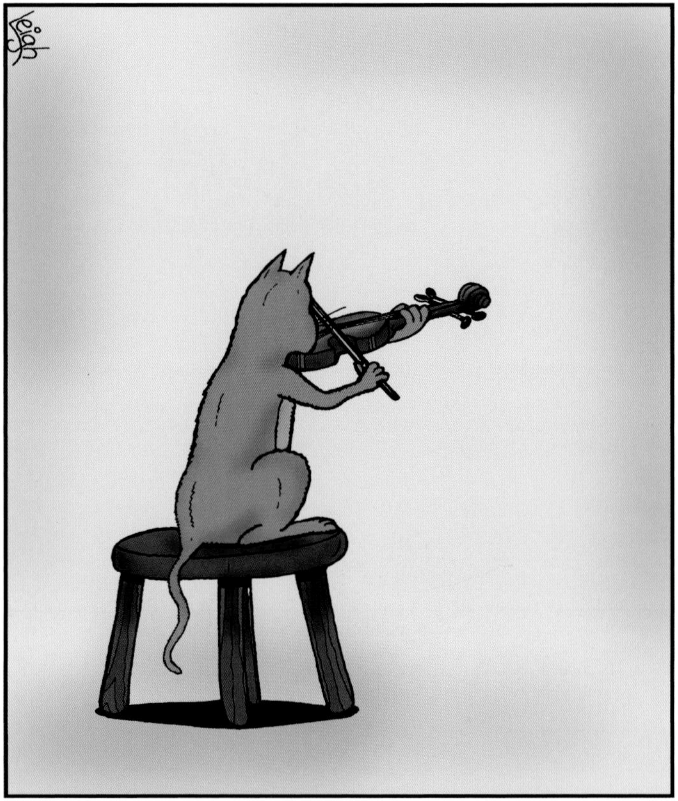

It was that rare quality that can only be described as gut instinct that made him naturally cut out for the string section.

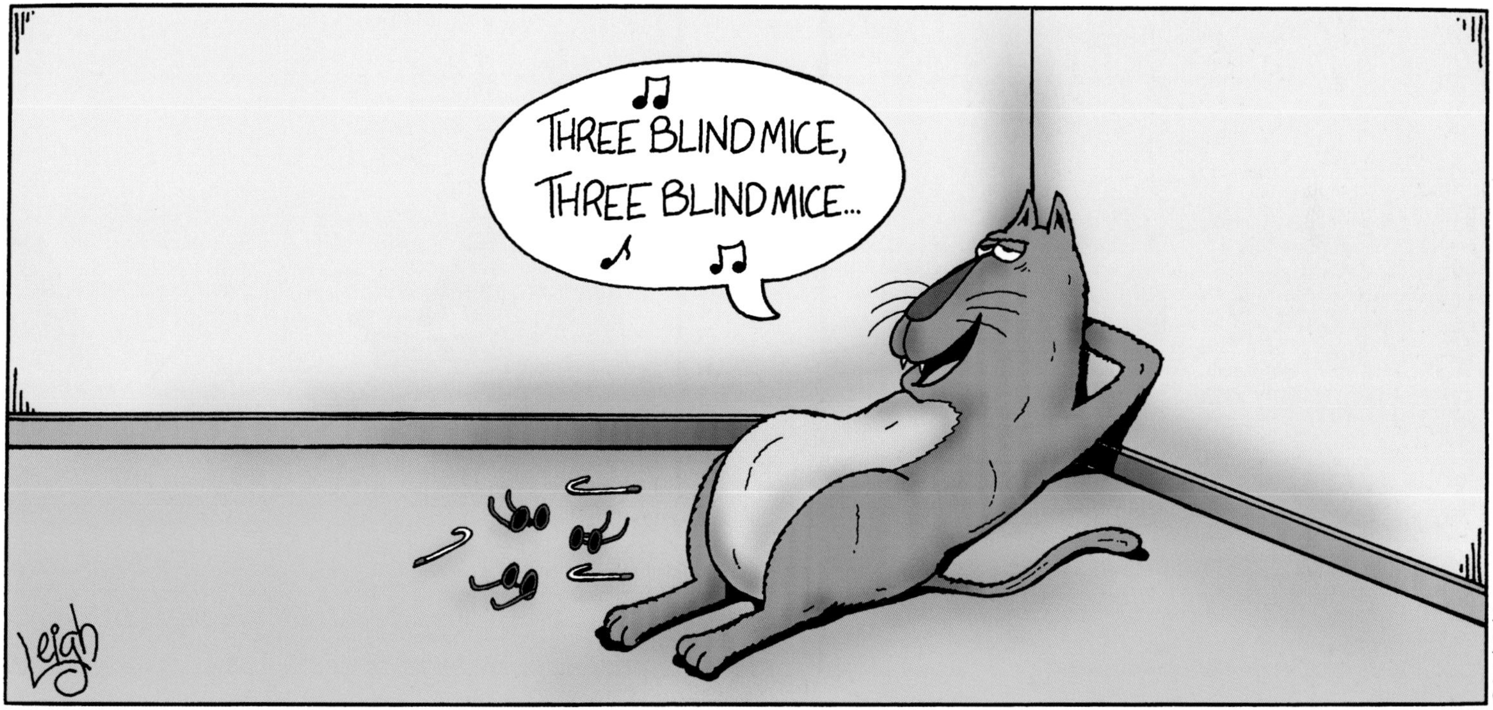
THREE BLIND MICE,
THREE BLIND MICE...
Leigh

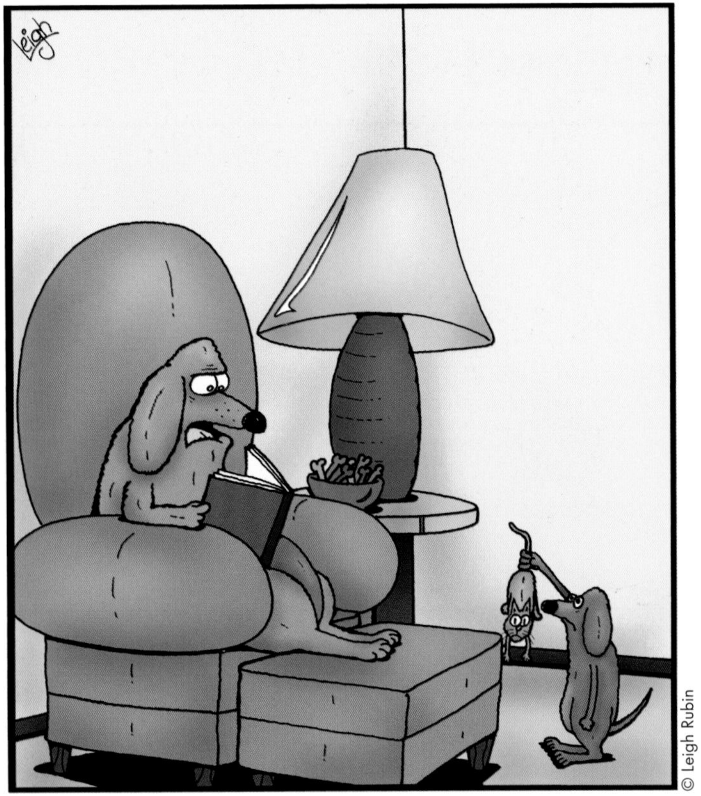
Leigh
© Leigh Rubin

"No, you may not have a kitten! You know the rules, no in-between meal snacks!"

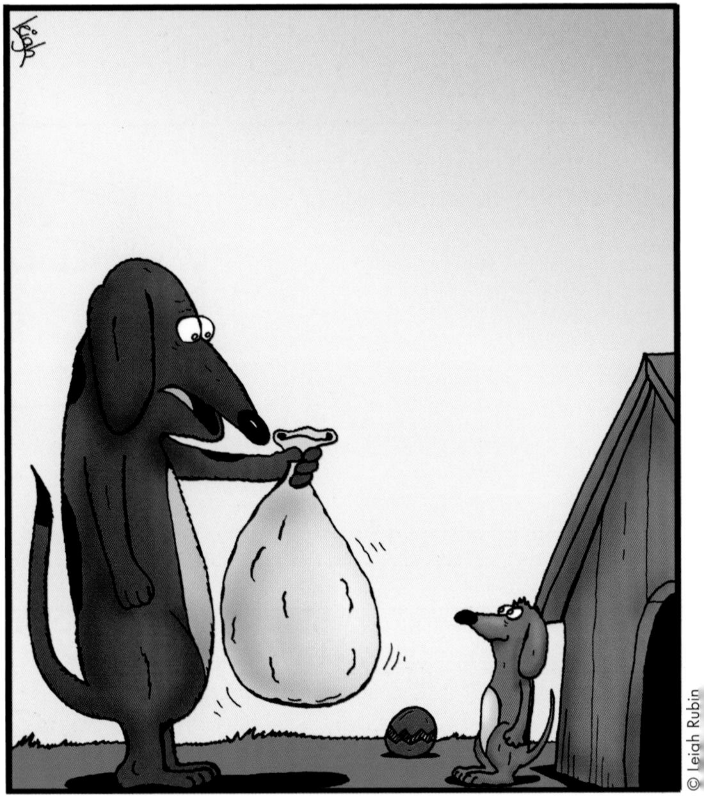
Leigh
© Leigh Rubin

"Now remember, son, this is a surprise for your mother. So whatever you do, don't let the cat out of the bag."

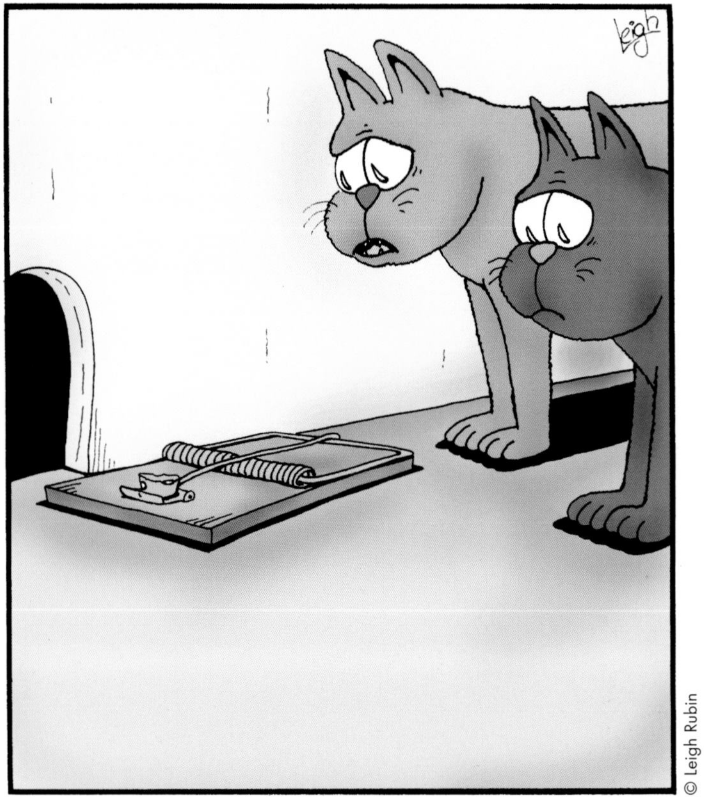
leigh
© Leigh Rubin

"Just as I feared... we're being replaced by modern technology."

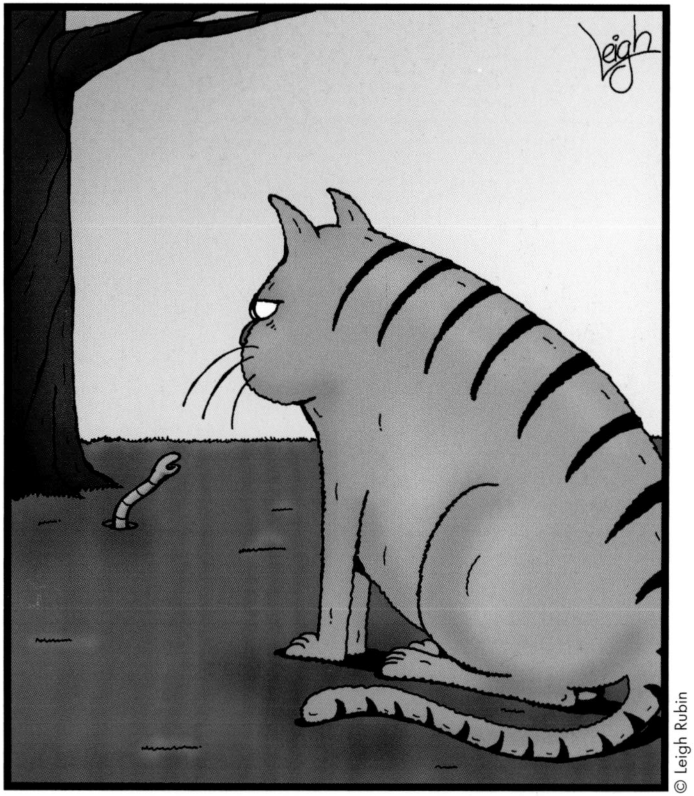
leigh
© Leigh Rubin

"Tomorrow morning, at 5:30 a.m. sharp, there'll be an early bird waiting outside this hole. ... That's where you come in."

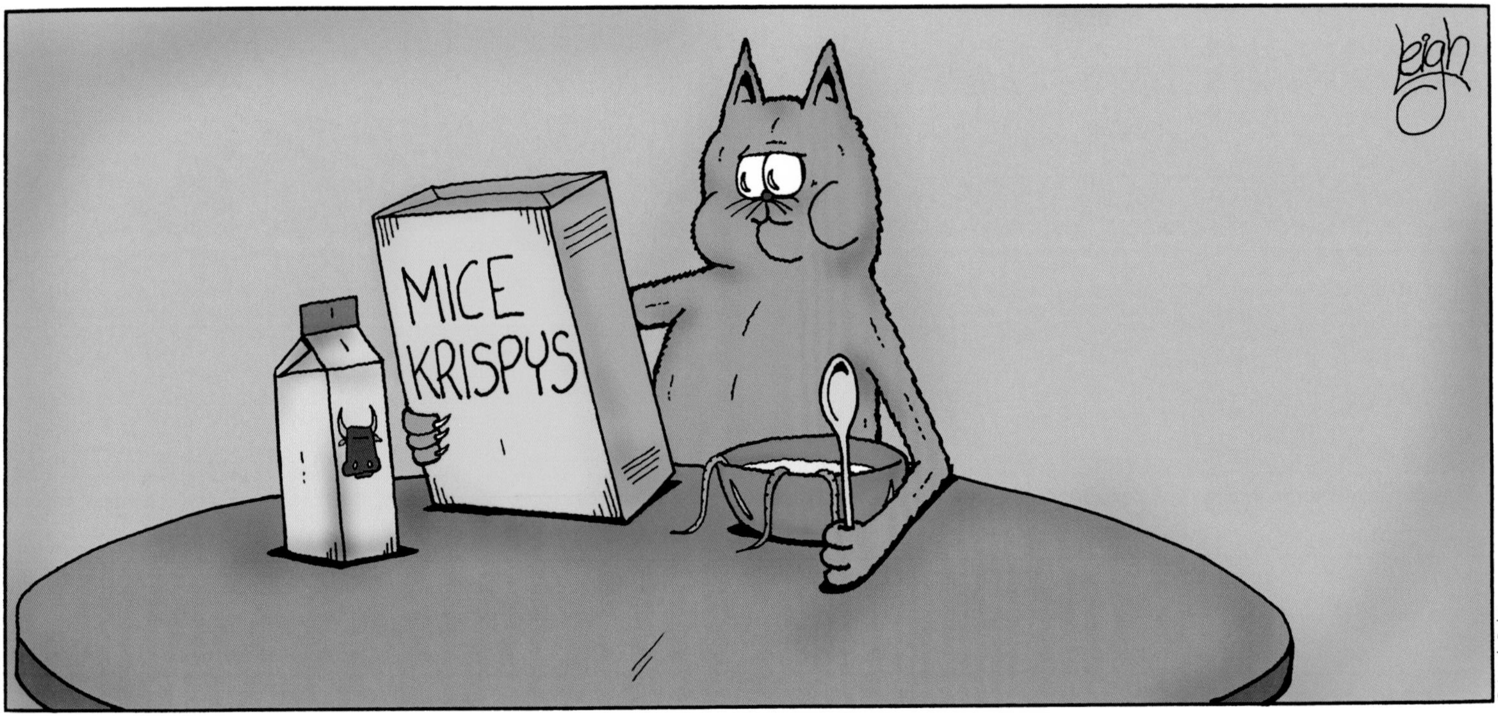
MICE
KRISPYS
Leigh

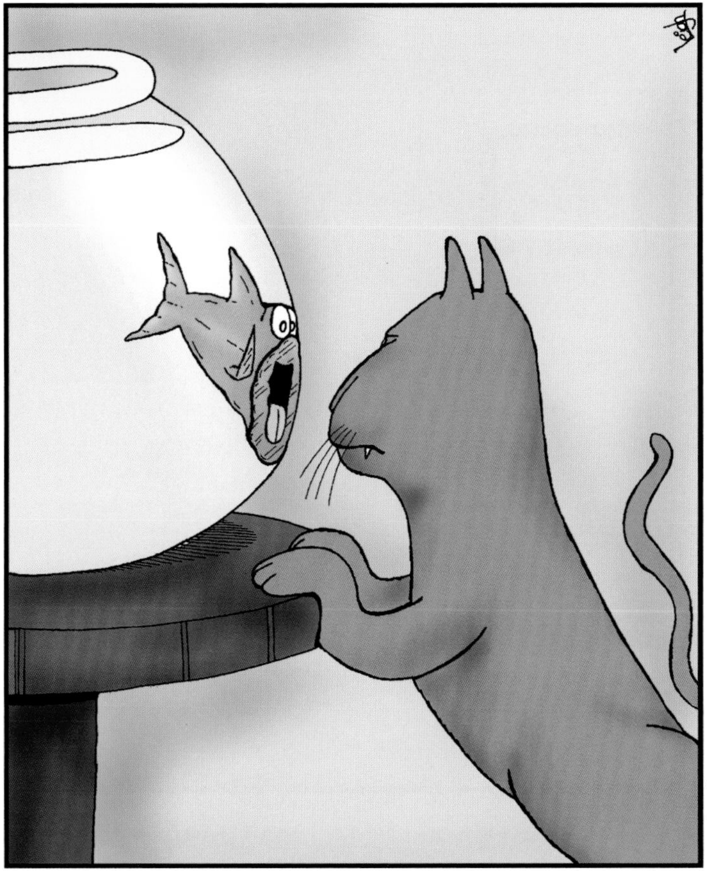

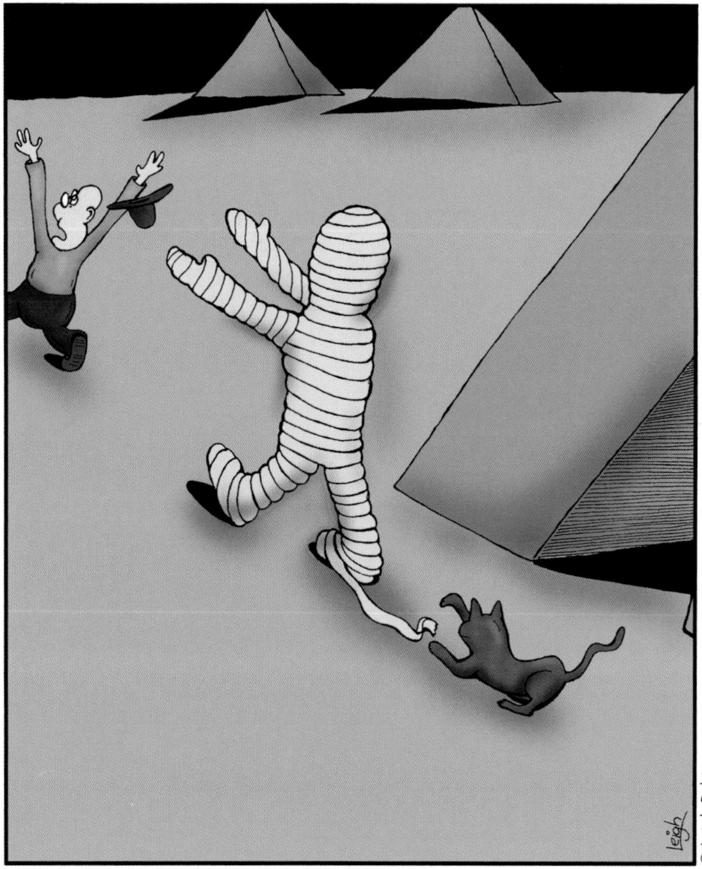

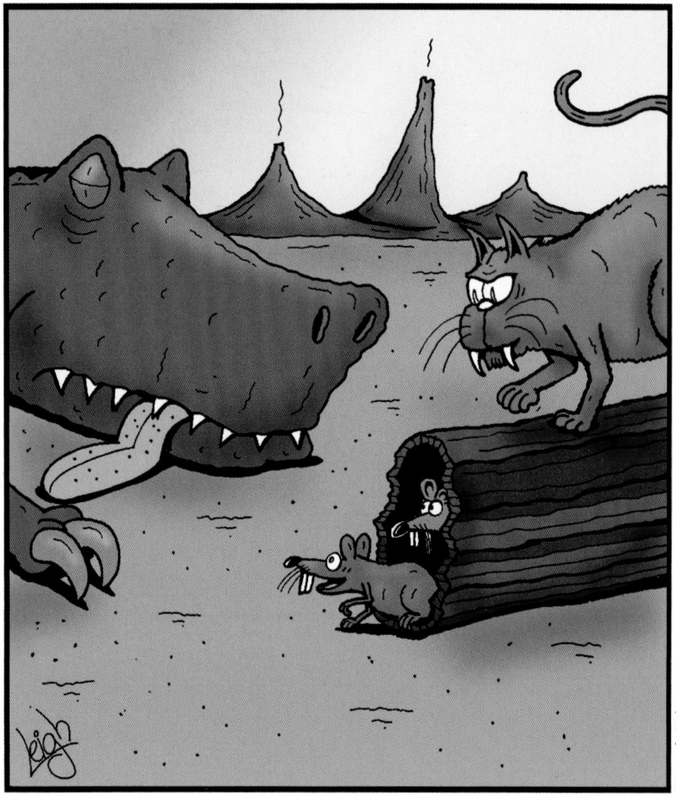

"Looks like that's the last of 'em, fellas.
We're safe at last!"

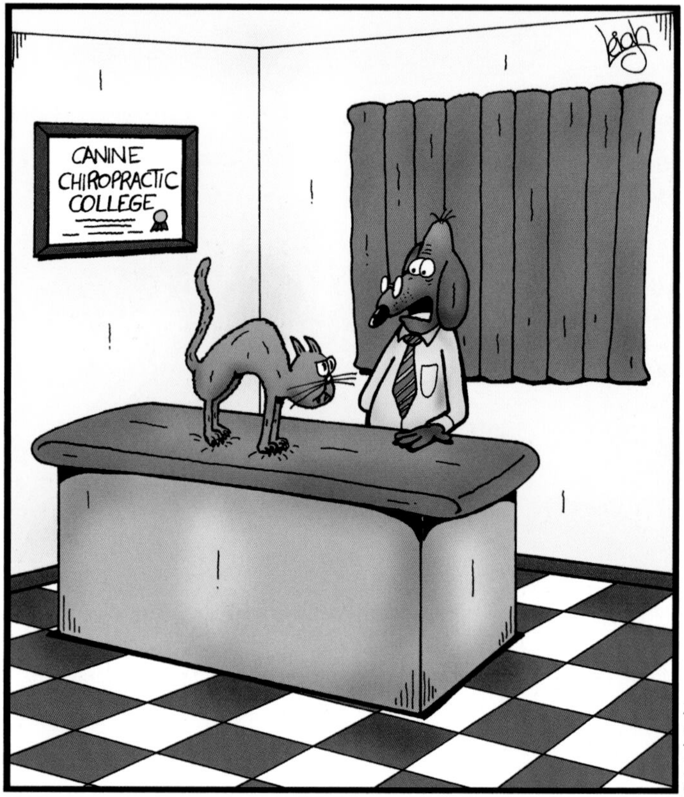
CANINE
CHIROPRACTIC
COLLEGE

© Leigh Rubin

"Now just try and relax. I can't possibly adjust your spine if you keep arching it at me like that!"

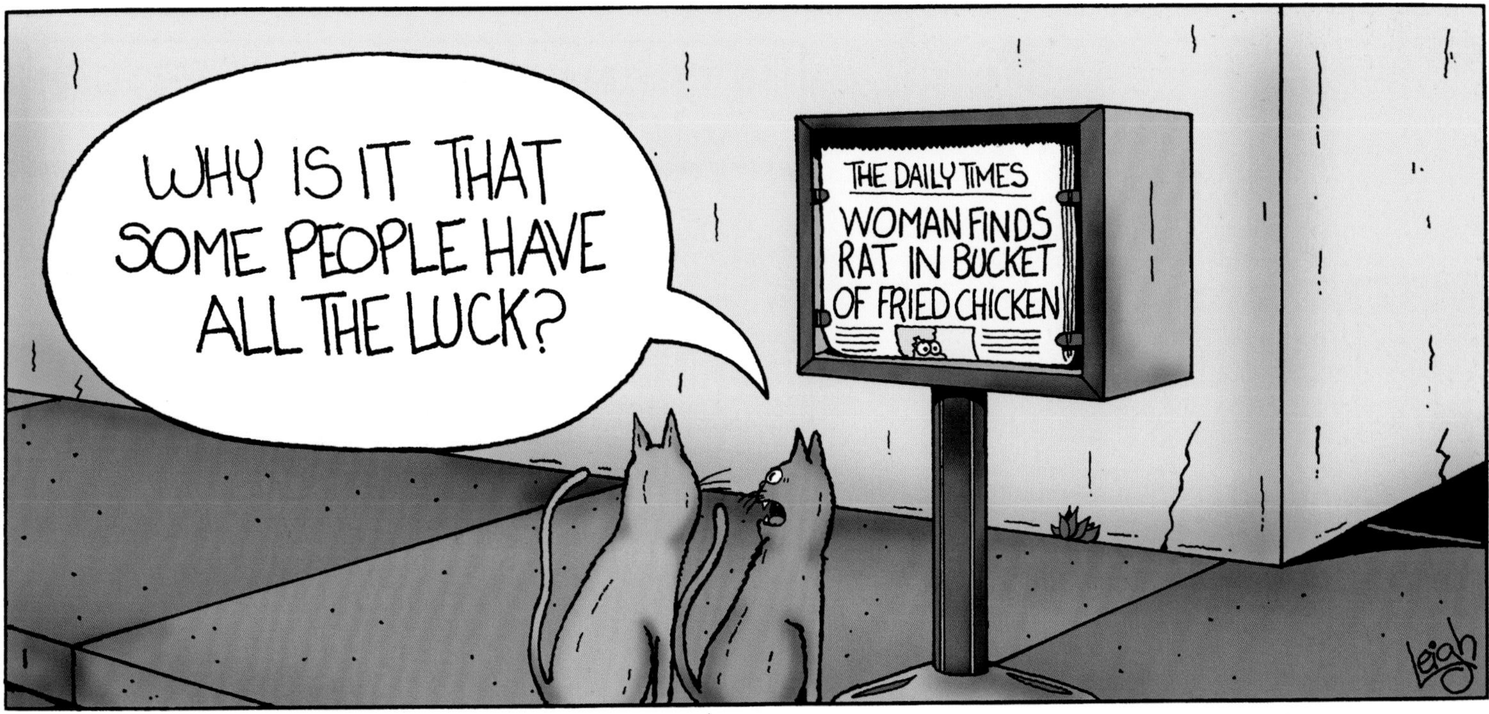
WHY IS IT THAT SOME PEOPLE HAVE ALL THE LUCK?
THE DAILY TIMES
WOMAN FINDS RAT IN BUCKET OF FRIED CHICKEN
Leigh

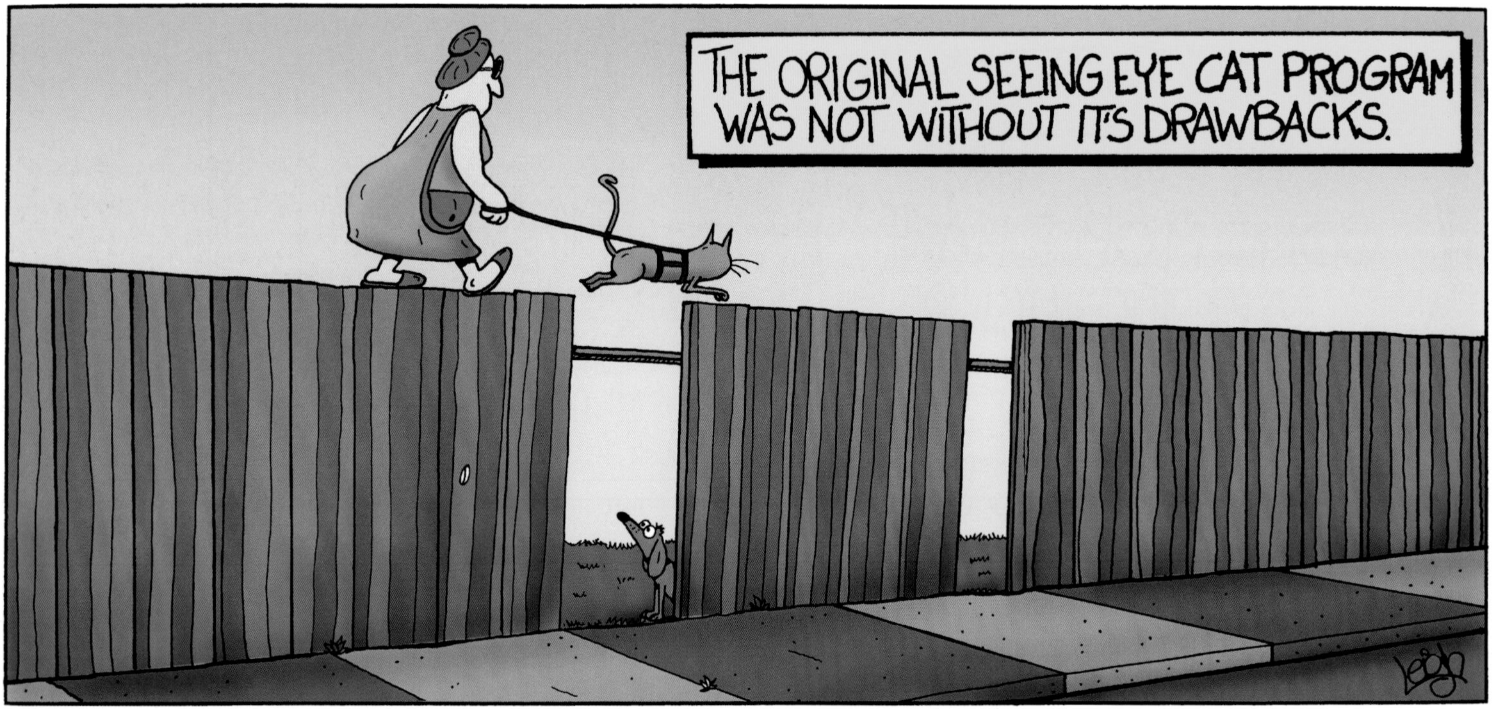
THE ORIGINAL SEEING EYE CAT PROGRAM WAS NOT WITHOUT IT'S DRAWBACKS.
leigh

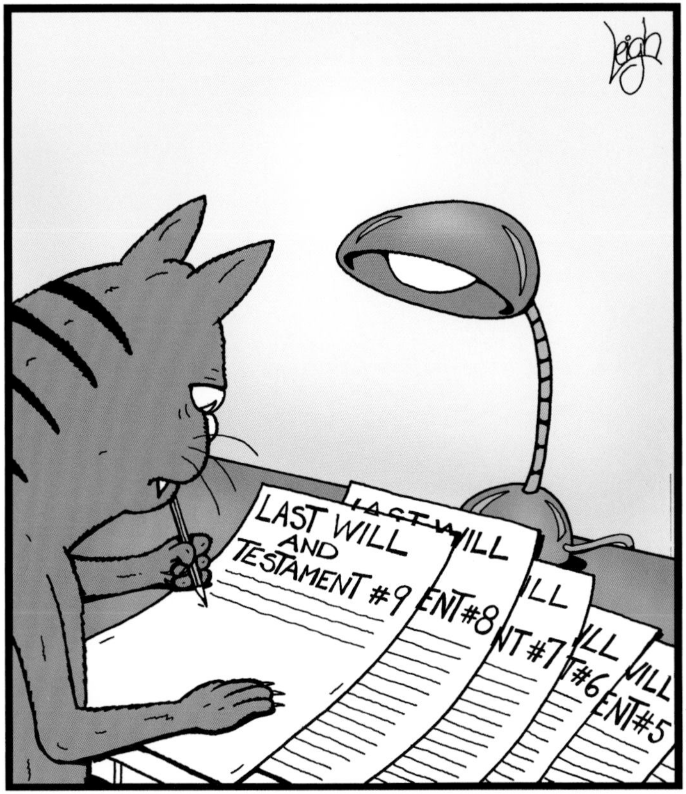
Leigh
LAST WILL
AND
TESTAMENT #9
ENT#8
NT#7
T#6
ENT#5

Why cats can't afford attorneys

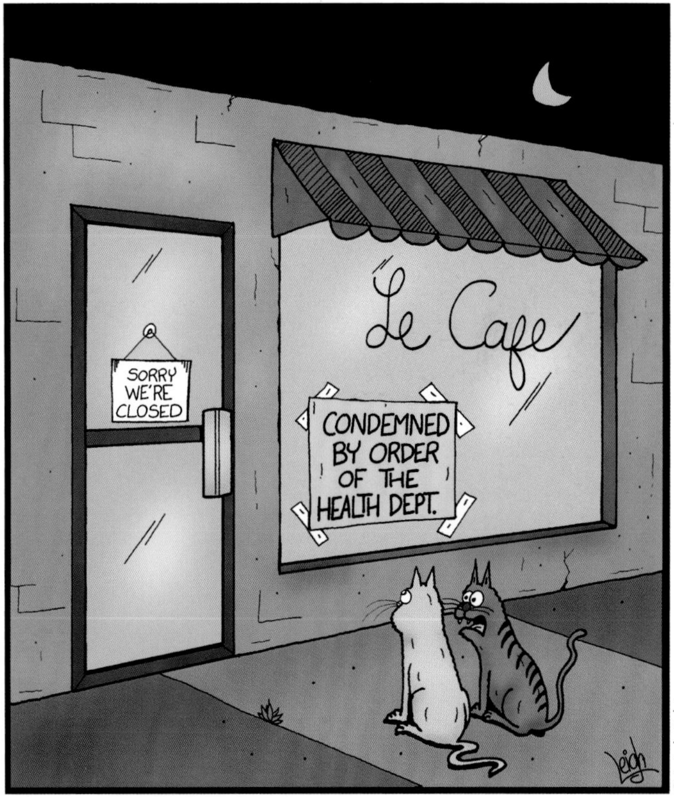
Le Cafe
SORRY
WE'RE
CLOSED
CONDEMNED
BY ORDER
OF THE
HEALTH DEPT.
Leigh

"It's a shame they had to close the place. I heard the rats here were just to ***die for***!"

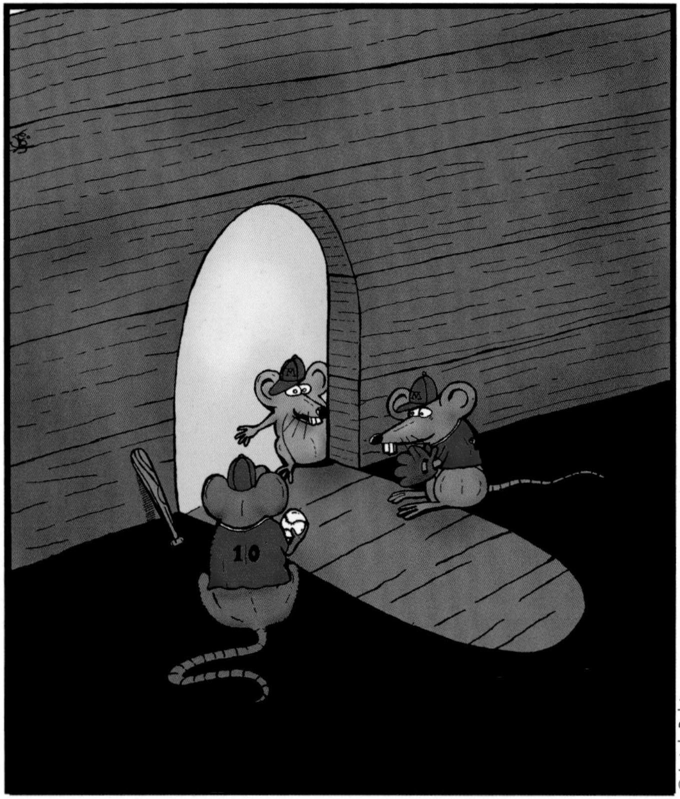
10

"It's cool, guys, the cat's away."

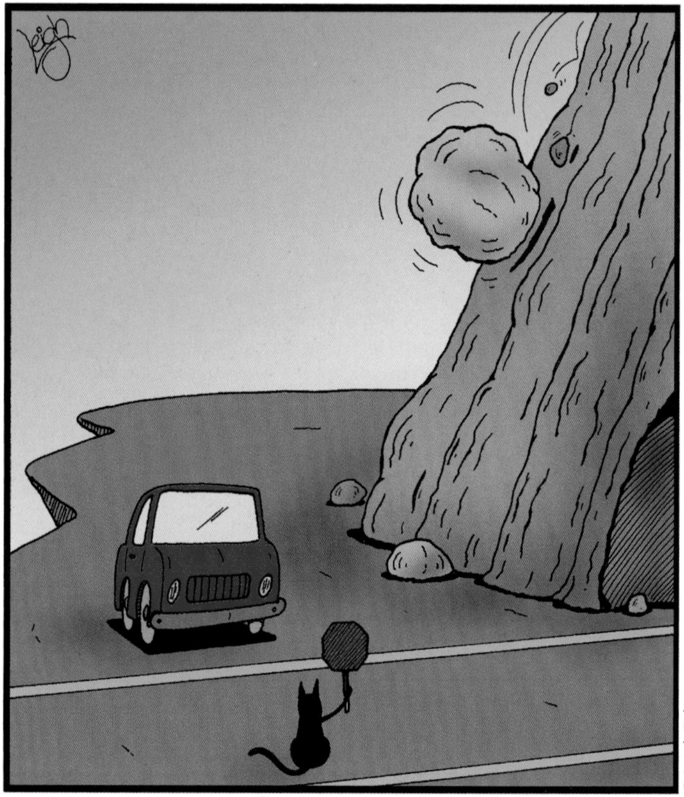

Black cat crossing guards

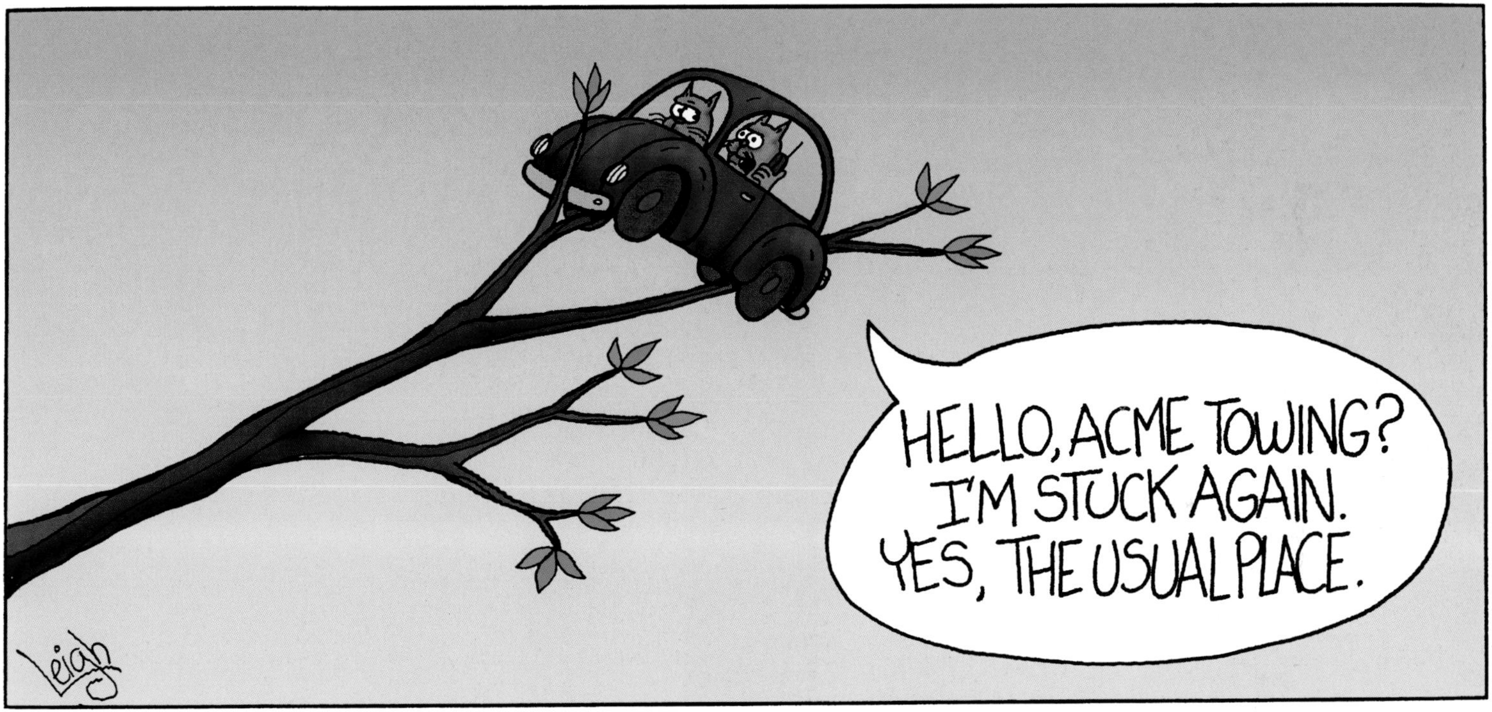
HELLO, ACME TOWING? I'M STUCK AGAIN. YES, THE USUAL PLACE.
Leigh

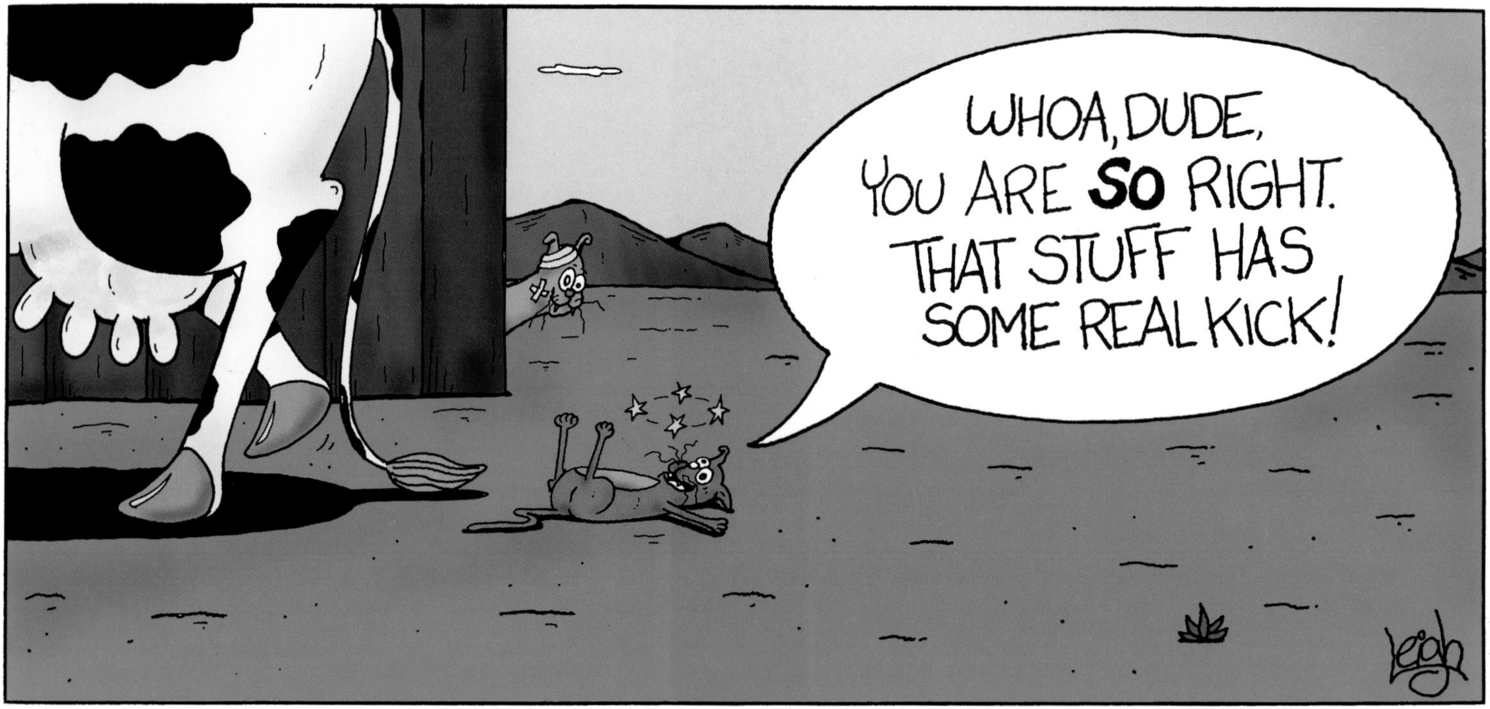
WHOA, DUDE,
YOU ARE **SO** RIGHT.
THAT STUFF HAS
SOME REAL KICK!
Leigh

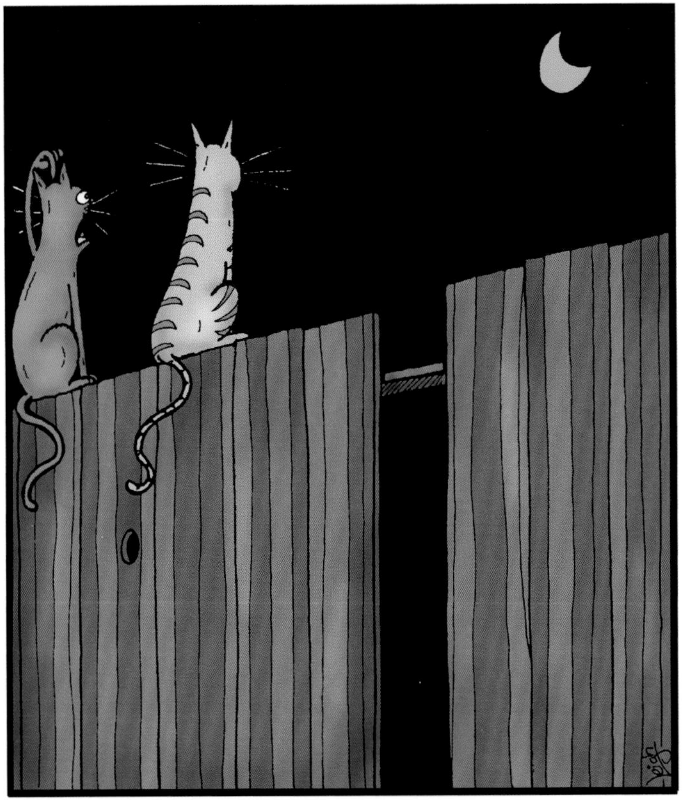

"Gee, Murray, I just don't know ... Do you think there are nine more lives after death?

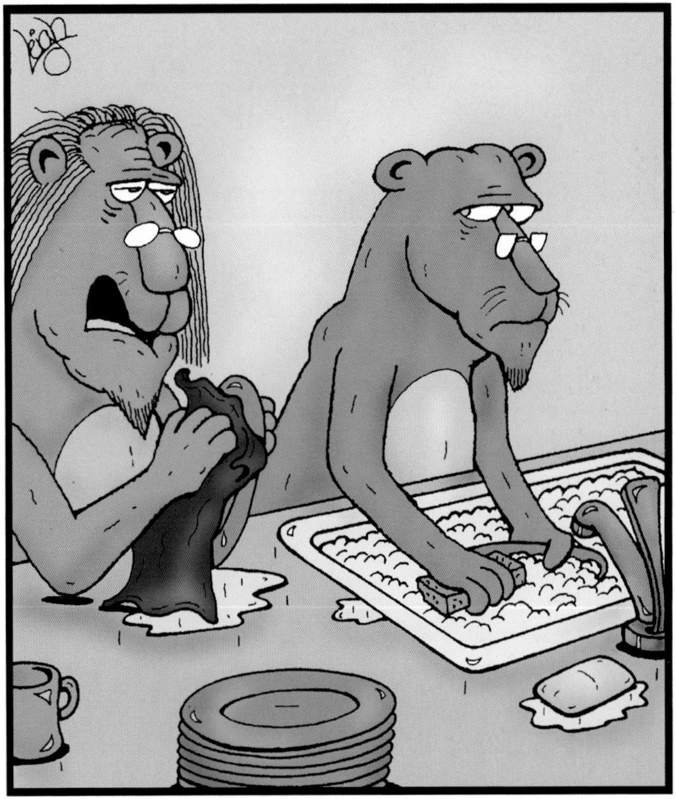

"What's happened to us, Edna? ... We used to be so *wild.*"

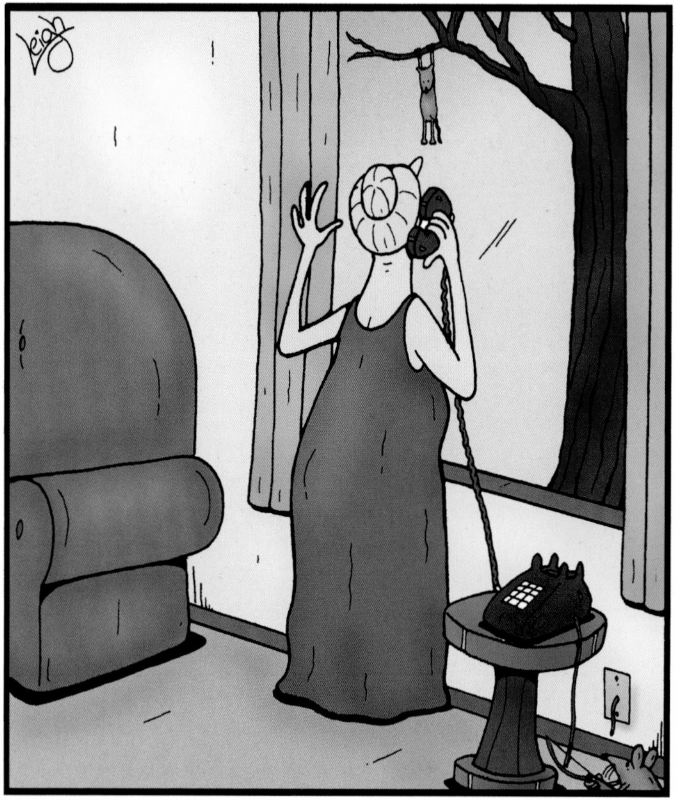
Leigh

© Leigh Rubin

"Hello, Fire Department?! Come quickly! My precious, little kitty's stuck up in a ... Hello? ... Fire Department? ... Hello?!"

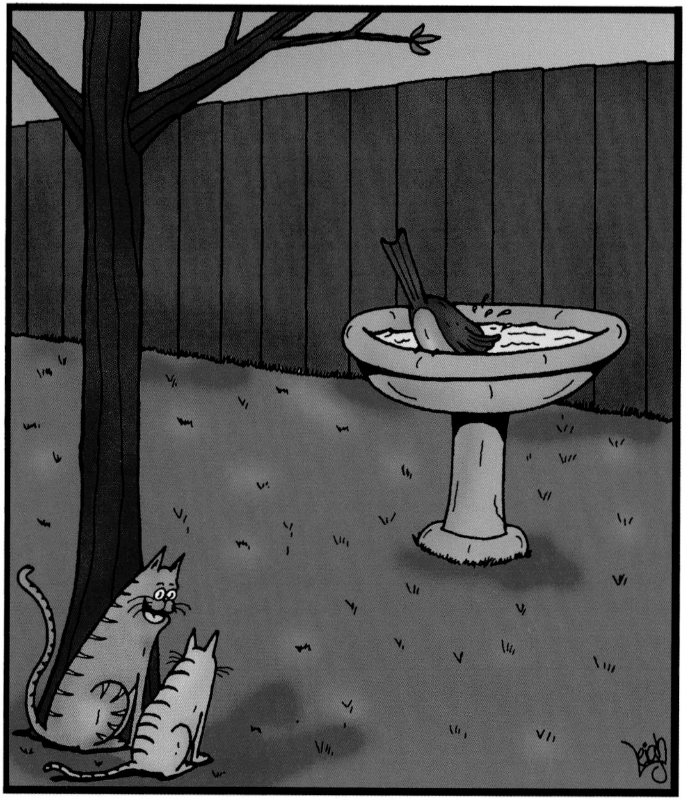
Leigh

© Leigh Rubin

"It's almost time to eat, honey. Why don't you go wash up for dinner while dinner washes up for you?"

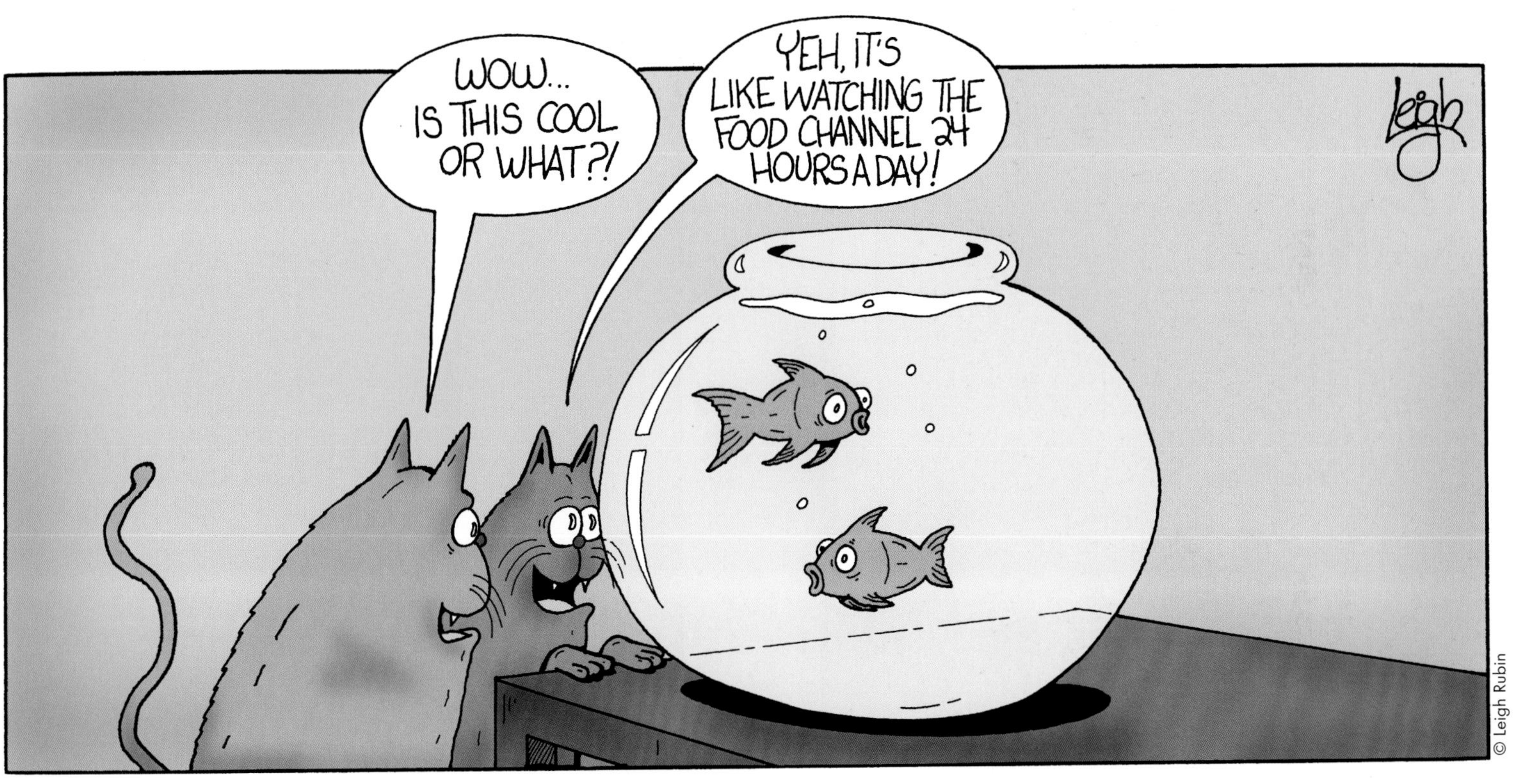
WOW... IS THIS COOL OR WHAT?!
YEH, IT'S LIKE WATCHING THE FOOD CHANNEL 24 HOURS A DAY!
Leigh
© Leigh Rubin

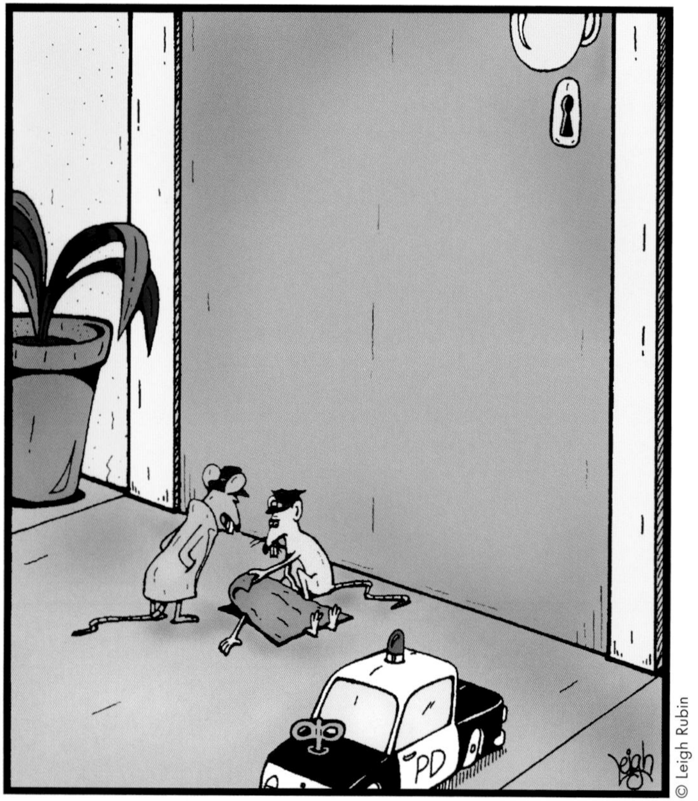
PD
Leigh
© Leigh Rubin

"Another horribly clawed victim, deliberately dumped at the front door. It's obviously the work of a psycho serial killer or some sicko copycat."

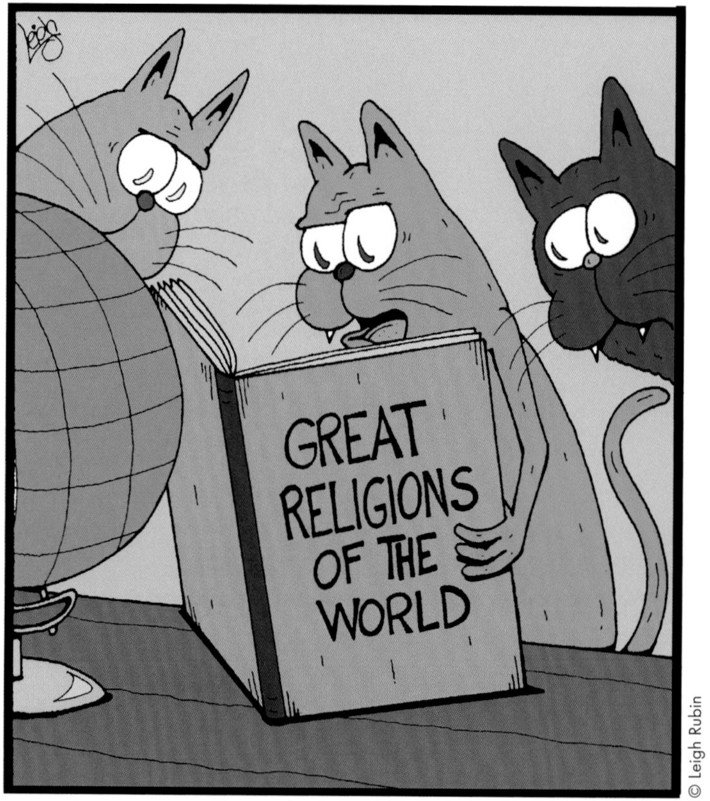
Leigh
GREAT RELIGIONS OF THE WORLD
© Leigh Rubin

"This is obviously a case of blatant discrimination! Despite being fanatically worshiped around the world, there's not a single mention of us in here anywhere!"

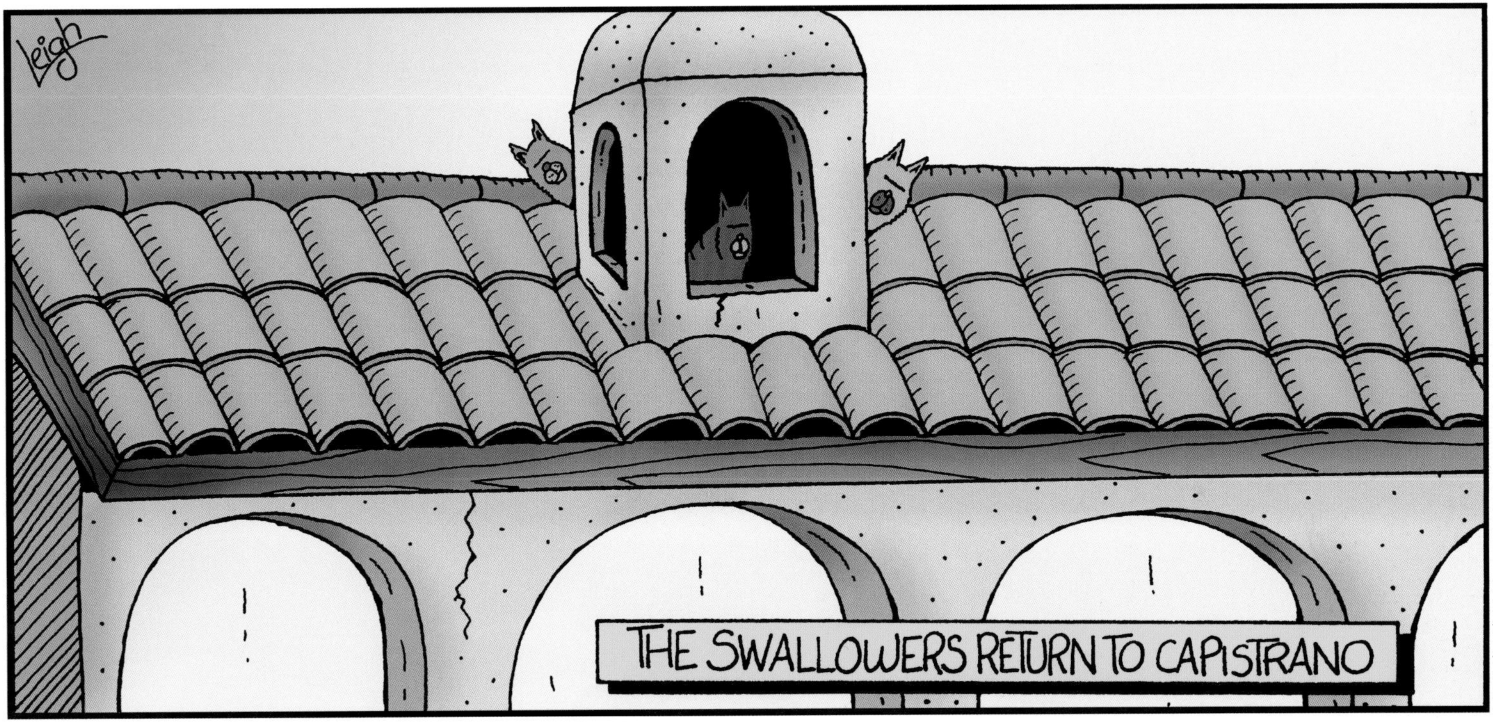
Leigh
THE SWALLOWERS RETURN TO CAPISTRANO

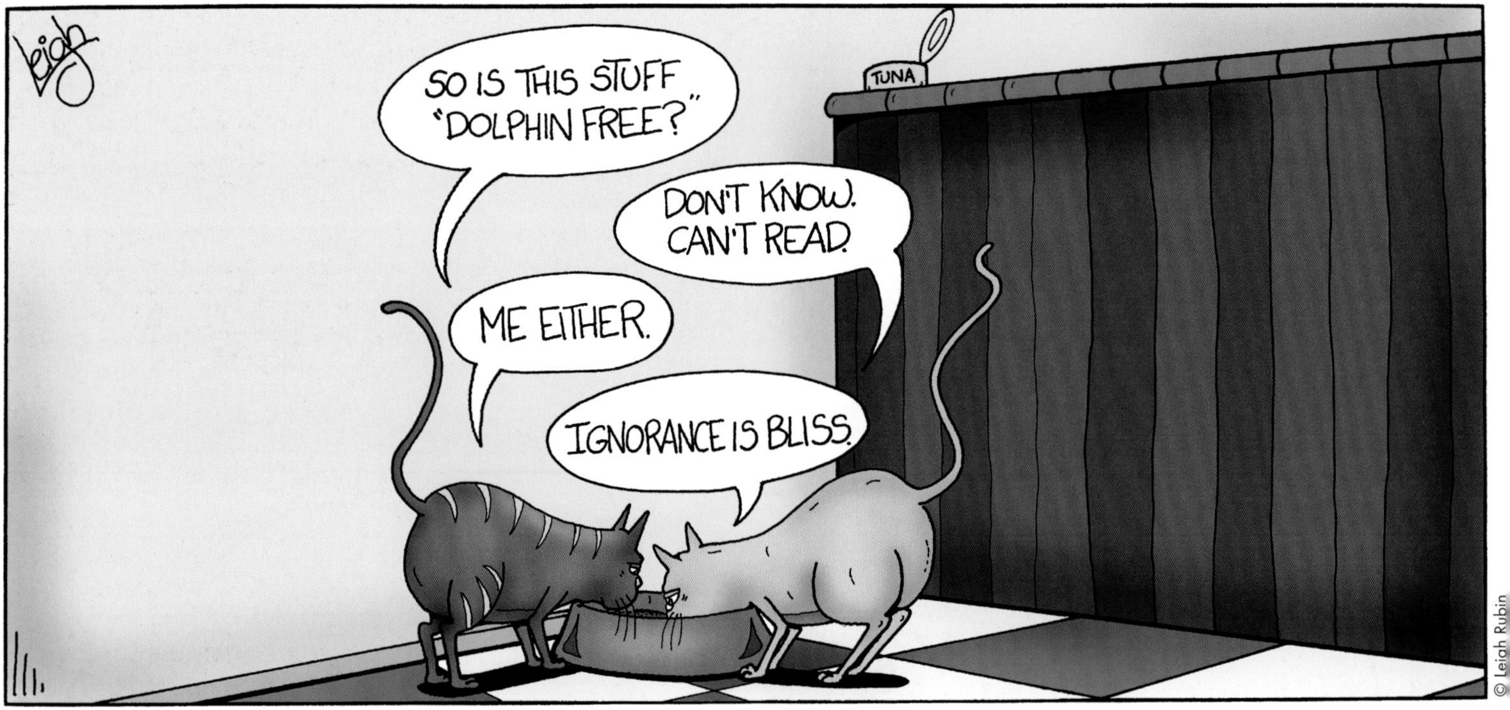
SO IS THIS STUFF "DOLPHIN FREE?"
DON'T KNOW. CAN'T READ.
ME EITHER.
IGNORANCE IS BLISS.
TUNA
© Leigh Rubin

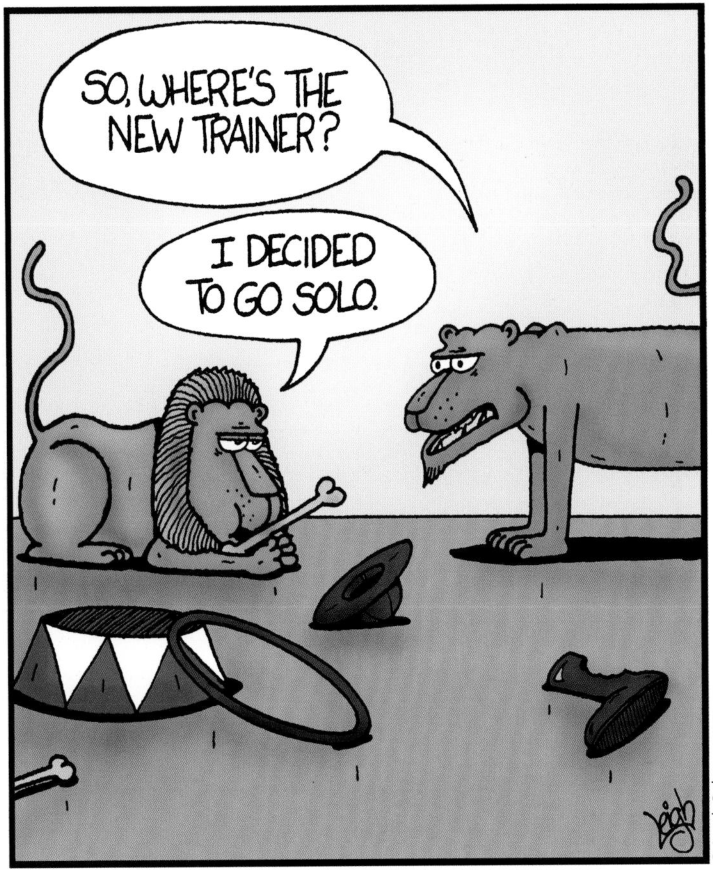
SO, WHERE'S THE NEW TRAINER?
I DECIDED TO GO SOLO.
leigh

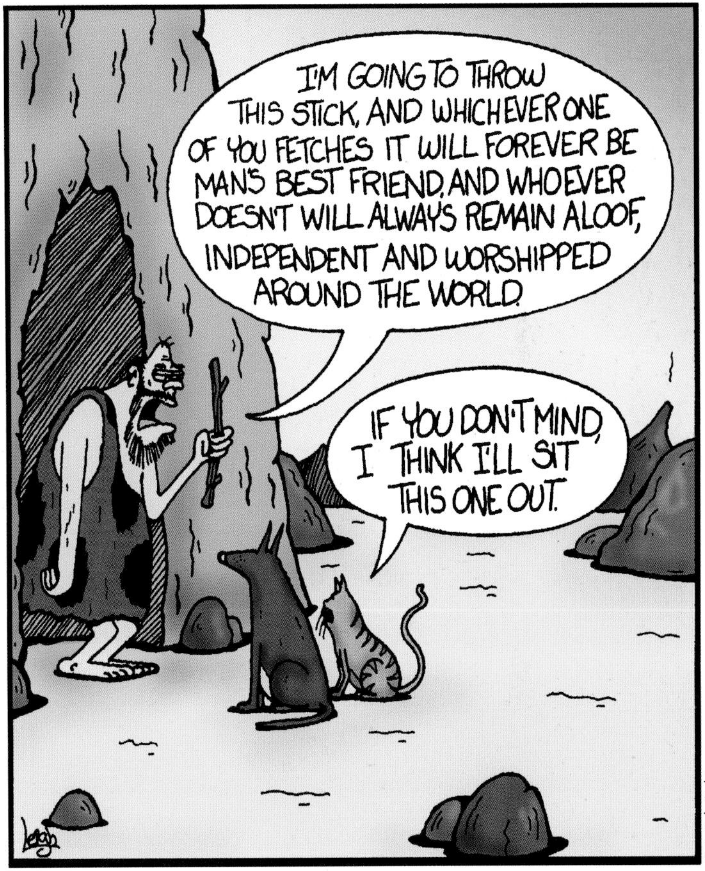
I'M GOING TO THROW THIS STICK, AND WHICHEVER ONE OF YOU FETCHES IT WILL FOREVER BE MAN'S BEST FRIEND, AND WHOEVER DOESN'T WILL ALWAYS REMAIN ALOOF, INDEPENDENT AND WORSHIPPED AROUND THE WORLD.
IF YOU DON'T MIND, I THINK I'LL SIT THIS ONE OUT.
leigh

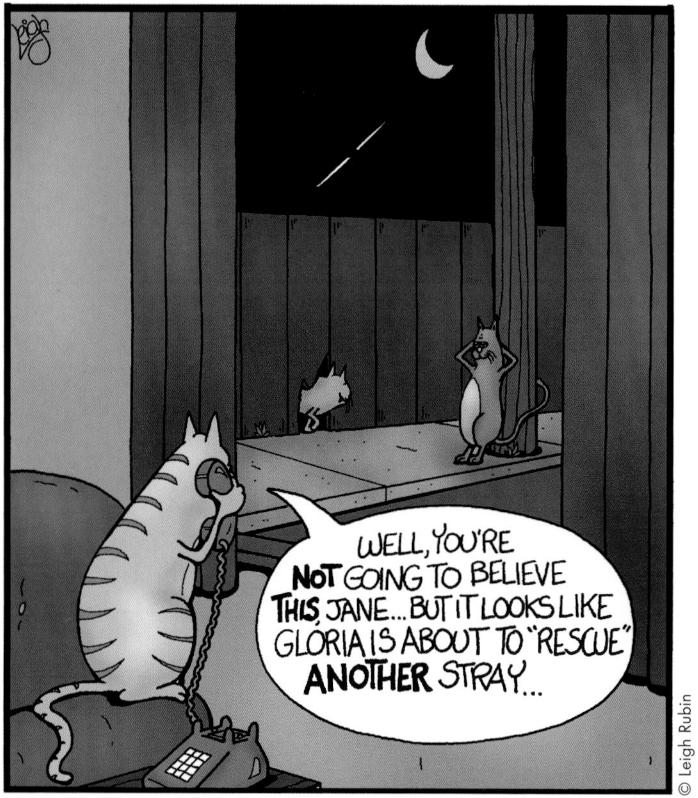
WELL, YOU'RE NOT GOING TO BELIEVE THIS, JANE... BUT IT LOOKS LIKE GLORIA IS ABOUT TO "RESCUE" ANOTHER STRAY...
© Leigh Rubin

Getting catty

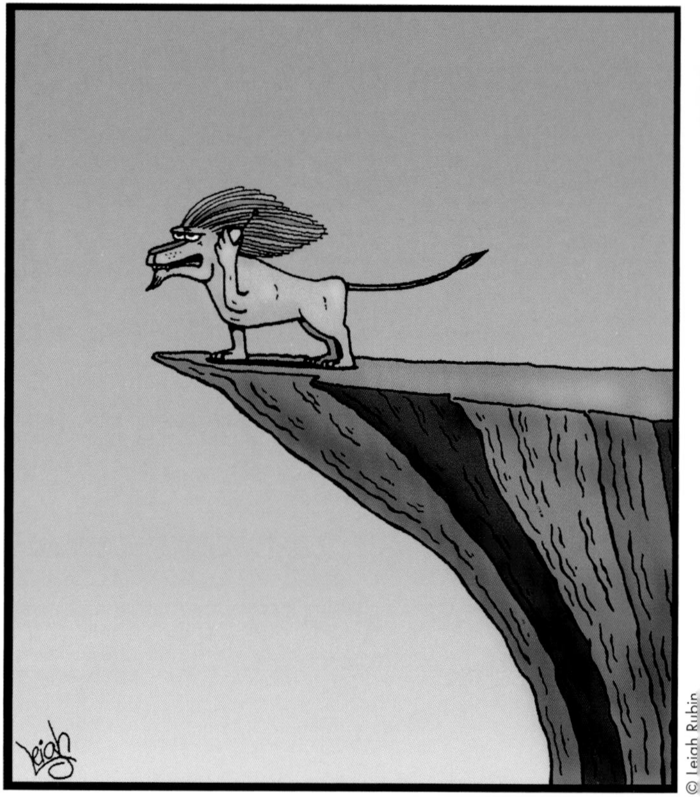
© Leigh Rubin

"... Why, I'm positively magnificent ...
And you?"

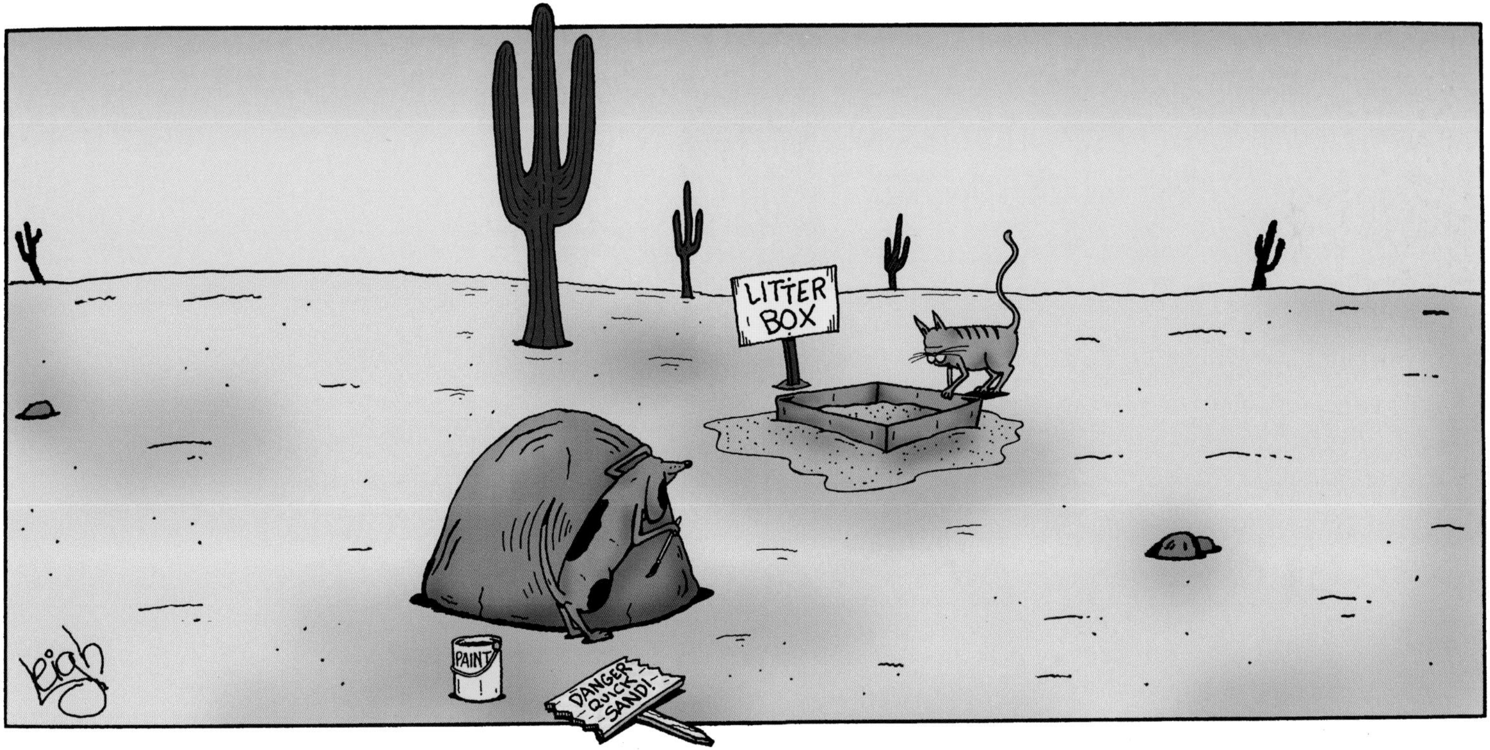
LITTER BOX
PAINT
DANGER QUICK SAND!
leigh

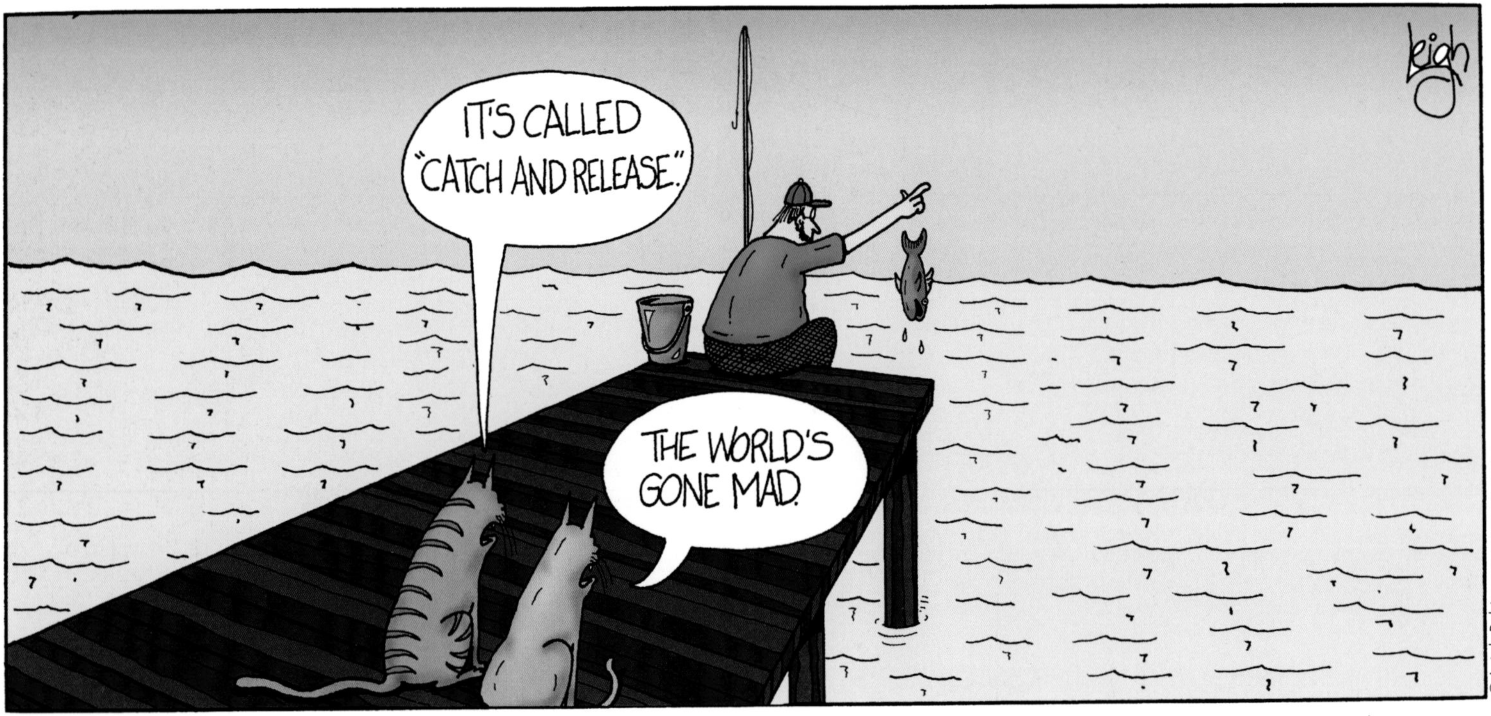
IT'S CALLED "CATCH AND RELEASE."
THE WORLD'S GONE MAD.
Leigh

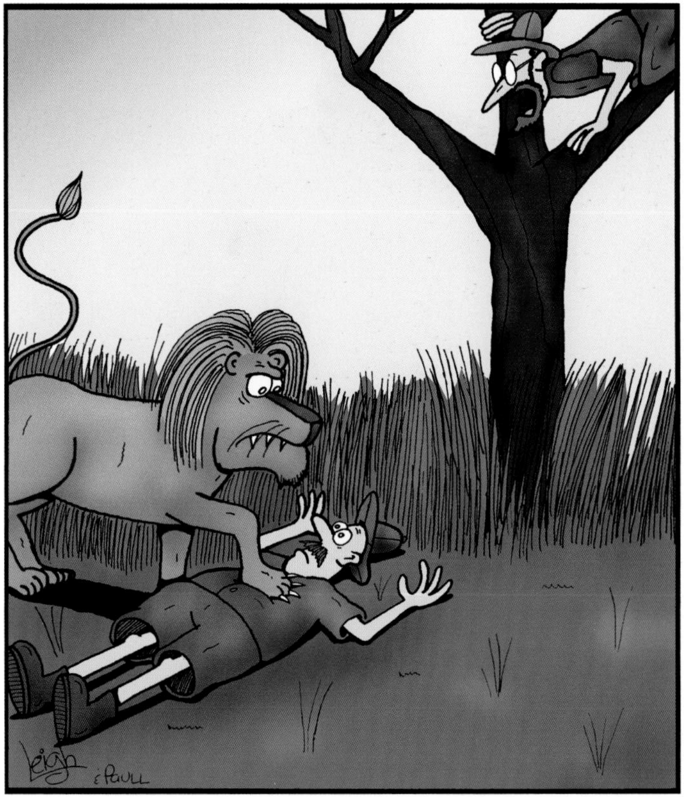
© Leigh Rubin

"I suppose this really puts that cat allergy of yours into perspective, eh, old boy?"

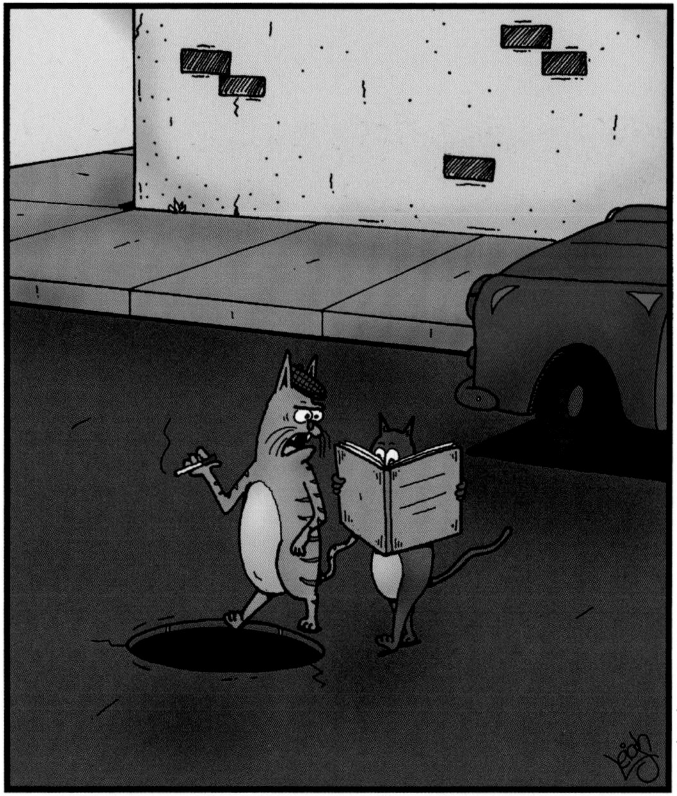
© Leigh Rubin

"That's the problem with you kids these days. You spend far too much time studying them books and not enough time developing your street smarts."

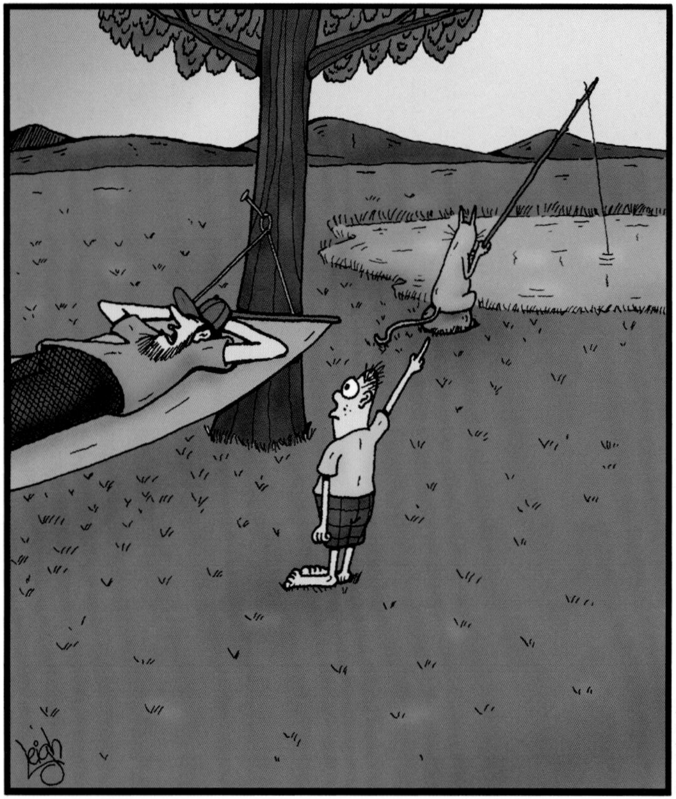
Leigh

"Calm down, boy, can't you see I'm tryin' to rest? ... Besides, what could possibly be so unusual about seein' a catfish?"

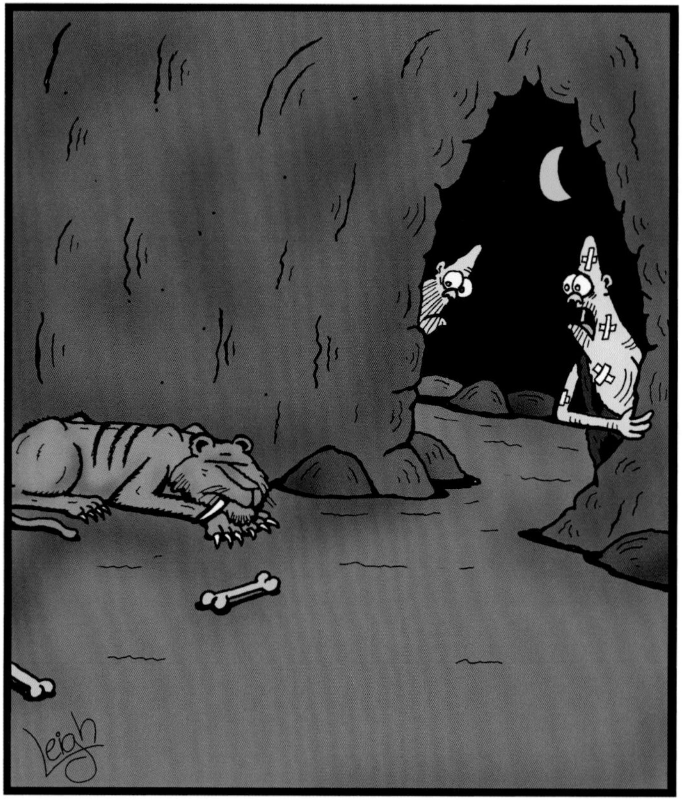
Leigh

"No way! It's *your* turn! *I* put the cat out *last* night!"

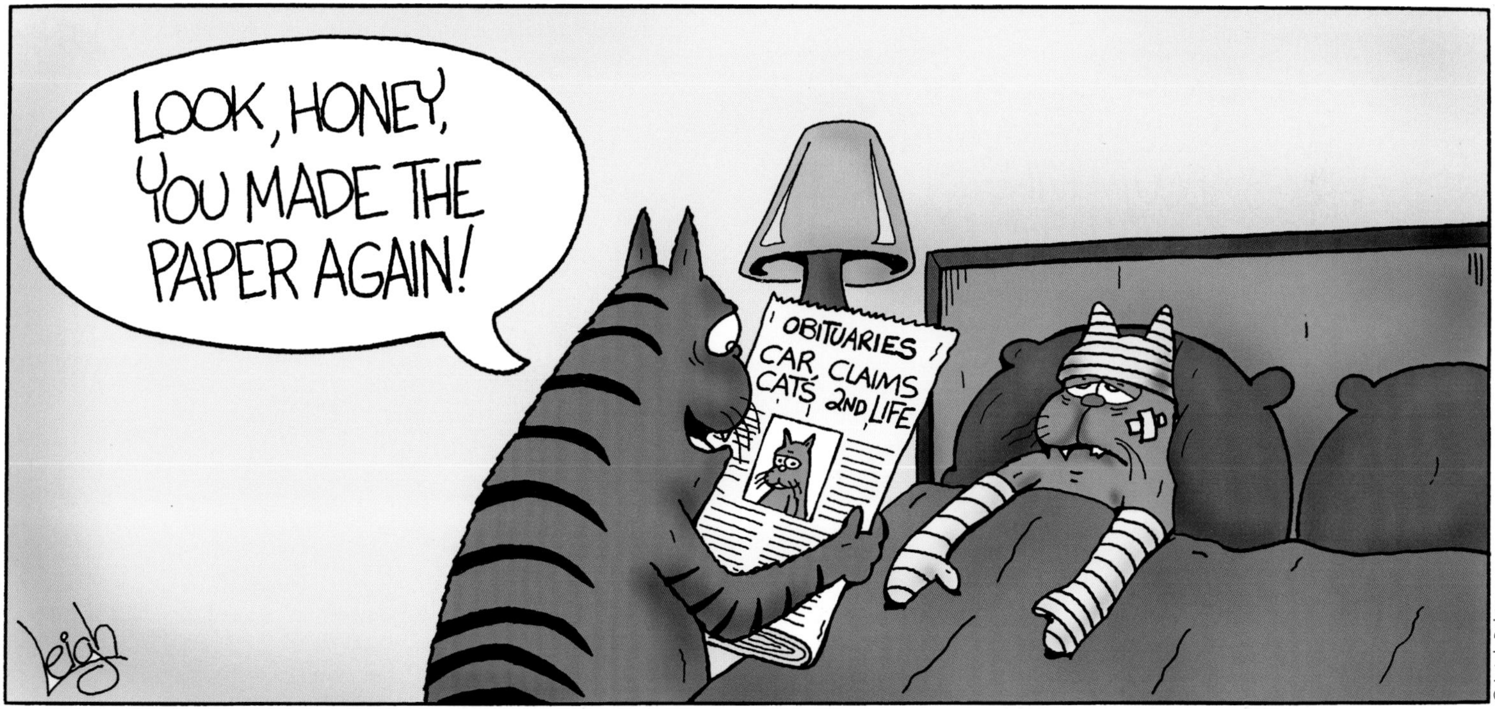
LOOK, HONEY, YOU MADE THE PAPER AGAIN!
OBITUARIES
CAR CLAIMS CAT'S 2ND LIFE
Leigh

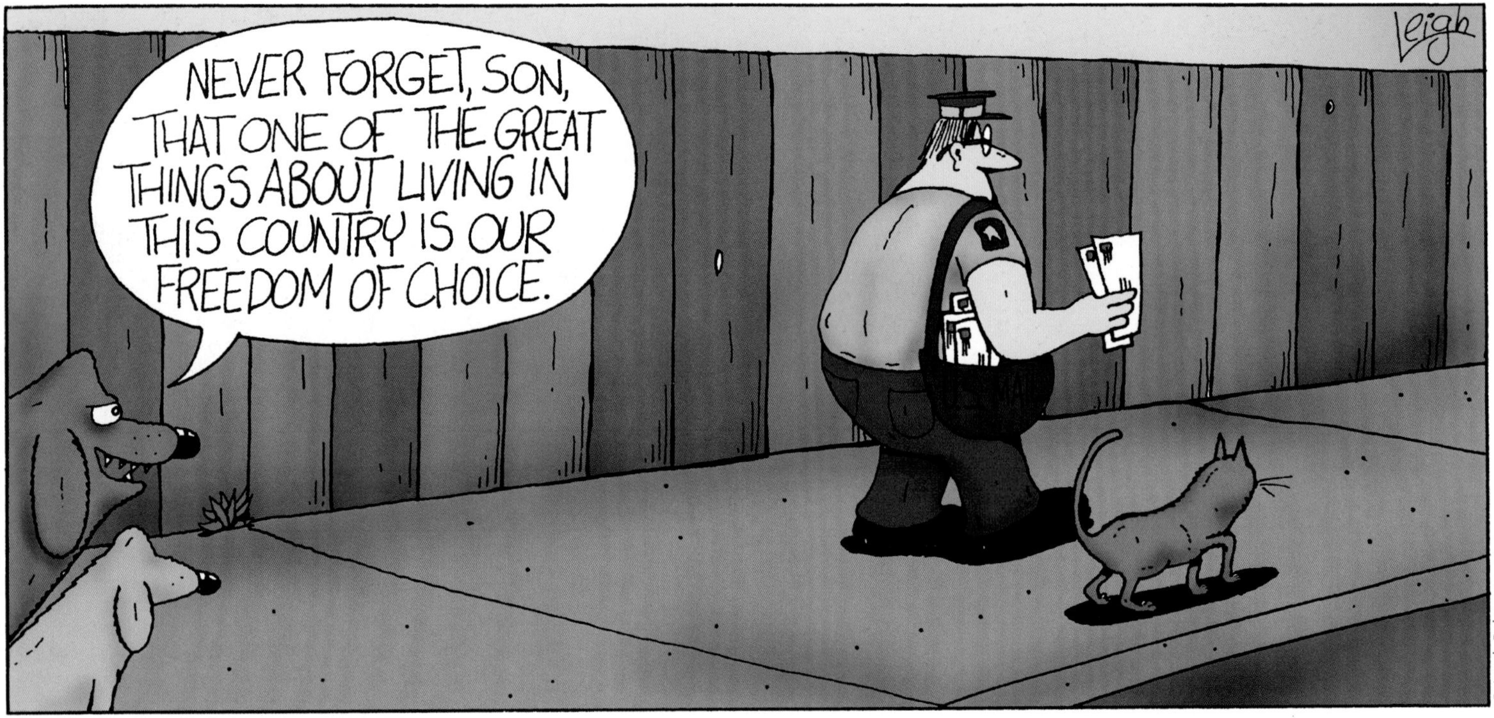
NEVER FORGET, SON, THAT ONE OF THE GREAT THINGS ABOUT LIVING IN THIS COUNTRY IS OUR FREEDOM OF CHOICE.
Leigh

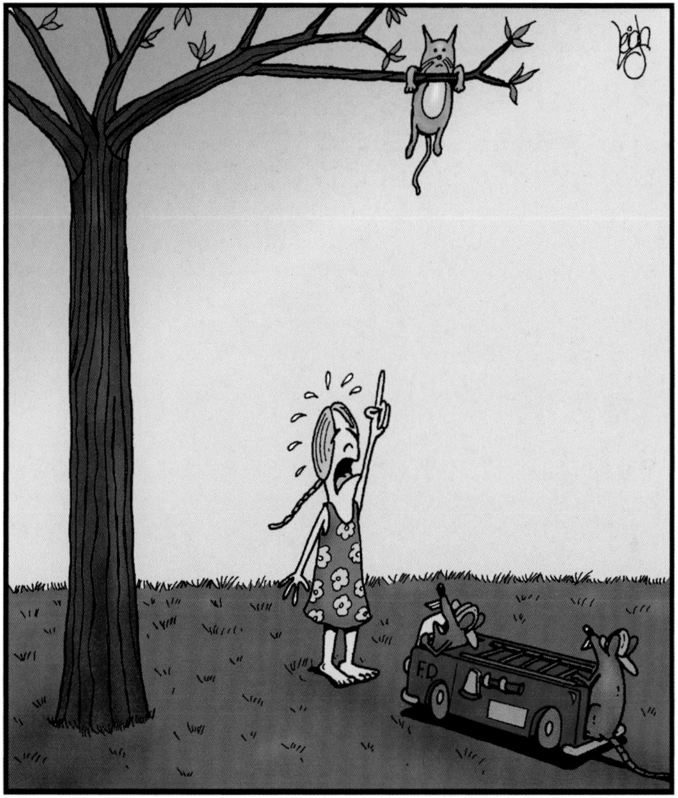
FD

"Well, this certainly poses a bit of an ethical dilemma, eh, Frank?"

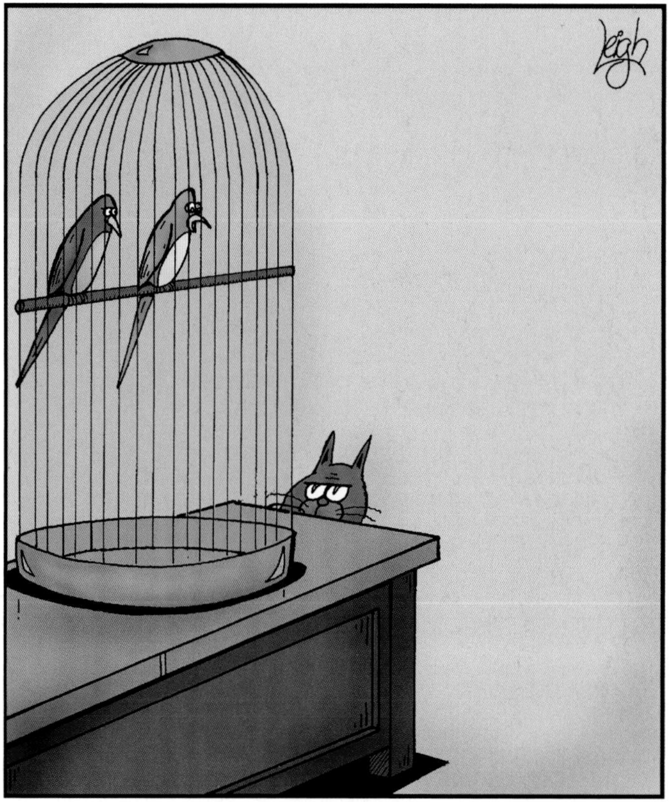

"Oh, sure, we have our security ... but at what price?"

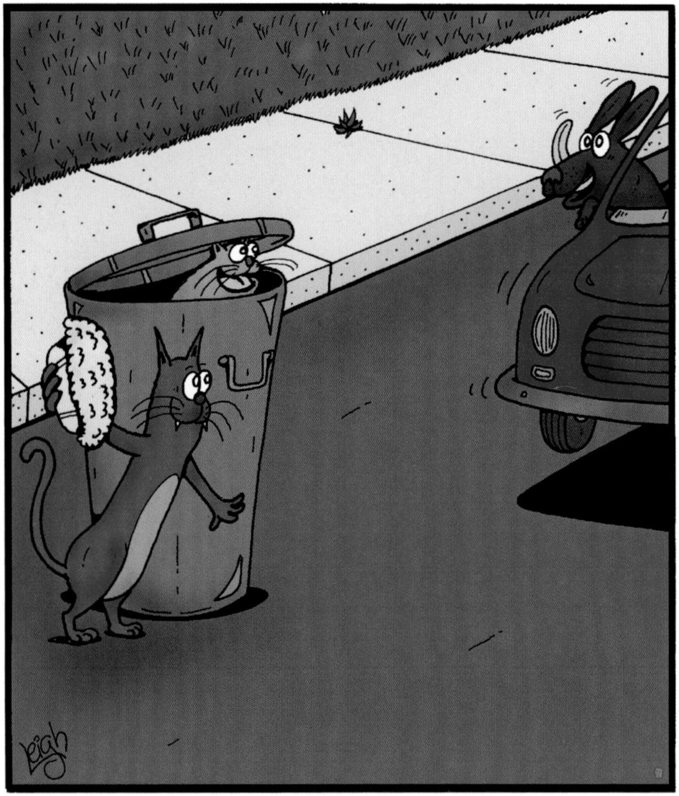

"... Five, four, three, two ... "

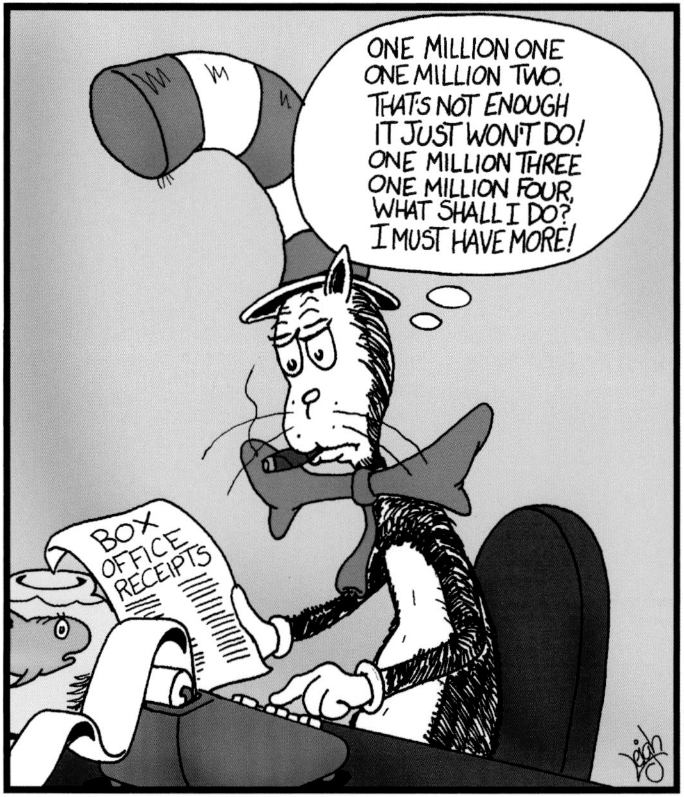
ONE MILLION ONE
ONE MILLION TWO.
THAT'S NOT ENOUGH
IT JUST WON'T DO!
ONE MILLION THREE
ONE MILLION FOUR,
WHAT SHALL I DO?
I MUST HAVE MORE!
BOX OFFICE RECEIPTS

The Fat Cat in the Hat

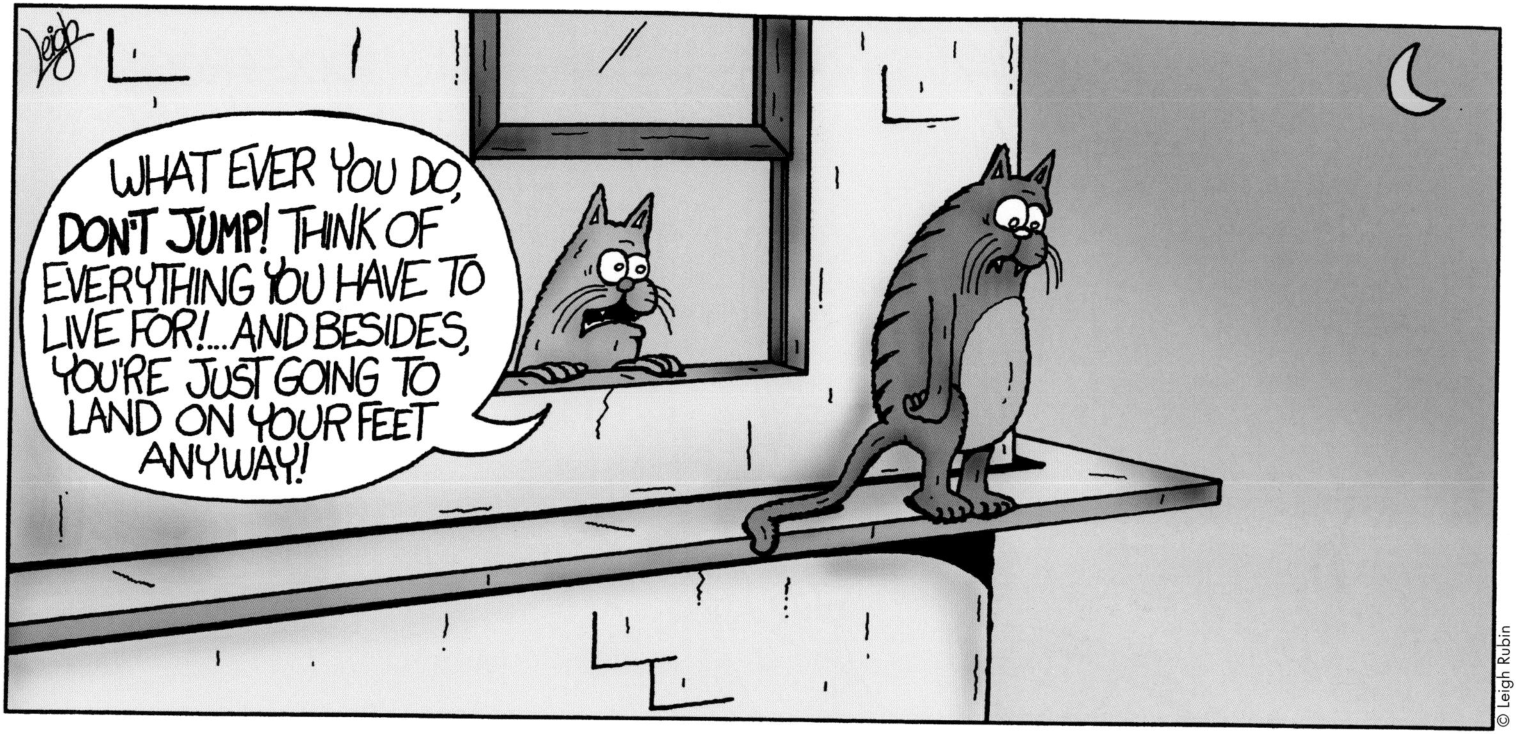
WHAT EVER YOU DO, DON'T JUMP! THINK OF EVERYTHING YOU HAVE TO LIVE FOR!...AND BESIDES, YOU'RE JUST GOING TO LAND ON YOUR FEET ANYWAY!
Leigh

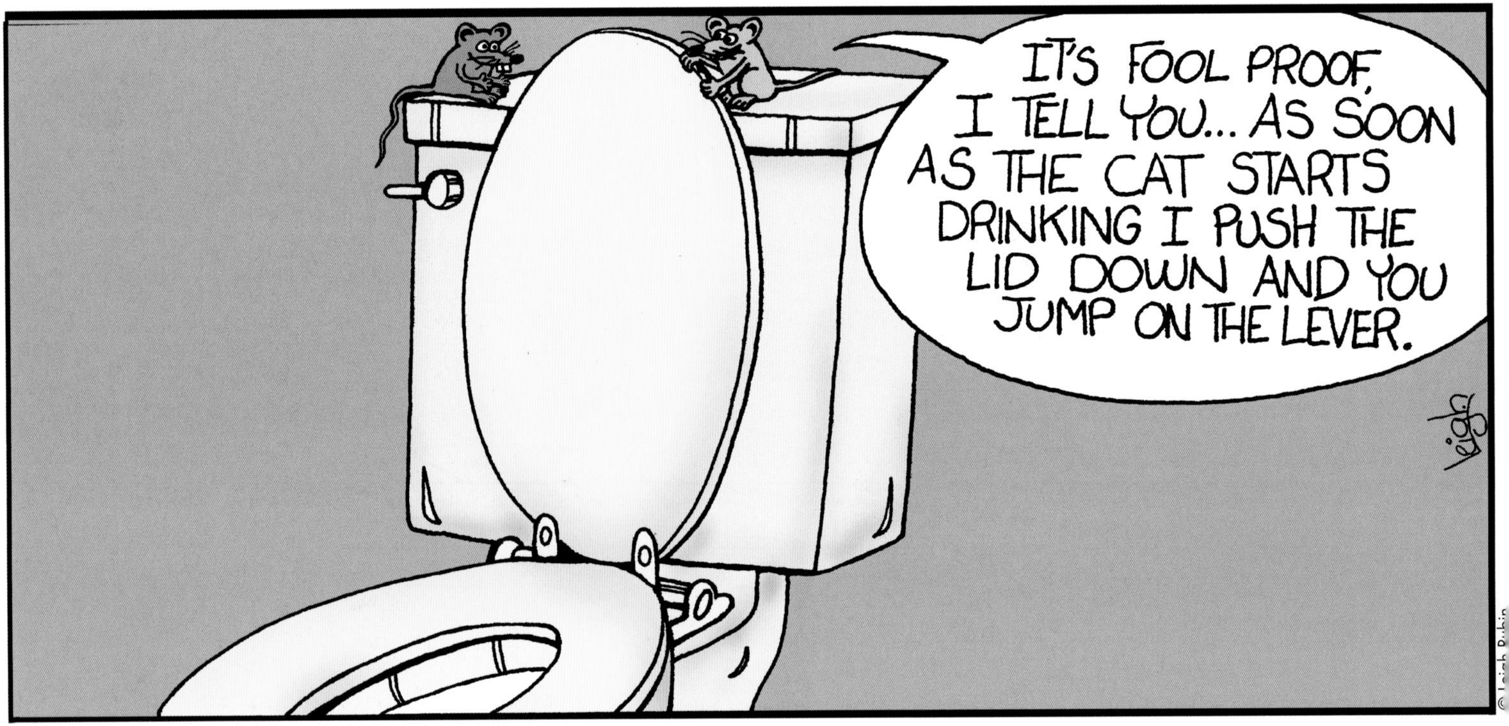
IT'S FOOL PROOF, I TELL YOU... AS SOON AS THE CAT STARTS DRINKING I PUSH THE LID DOWN AND YOU JUMP ON THE LEVER.
leigh
© Leigh Rubin

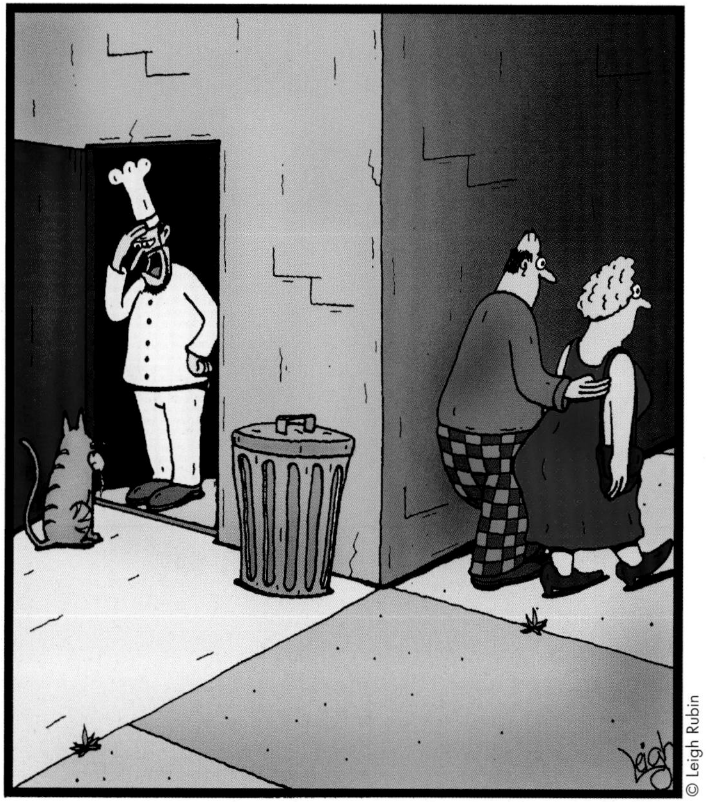
© Leigh Rubin

"No! No! No! How many times do I have to tell you? The recipe specifically calls for rats, not mice!"

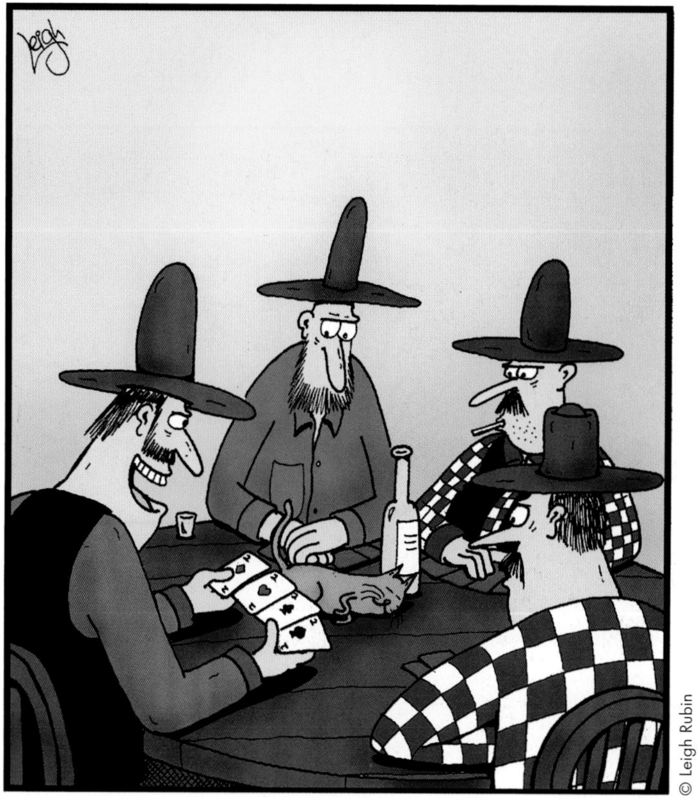
© Leigh Rubin

"Four of a kind, gentlemen. Looks like the kitty's all mine."

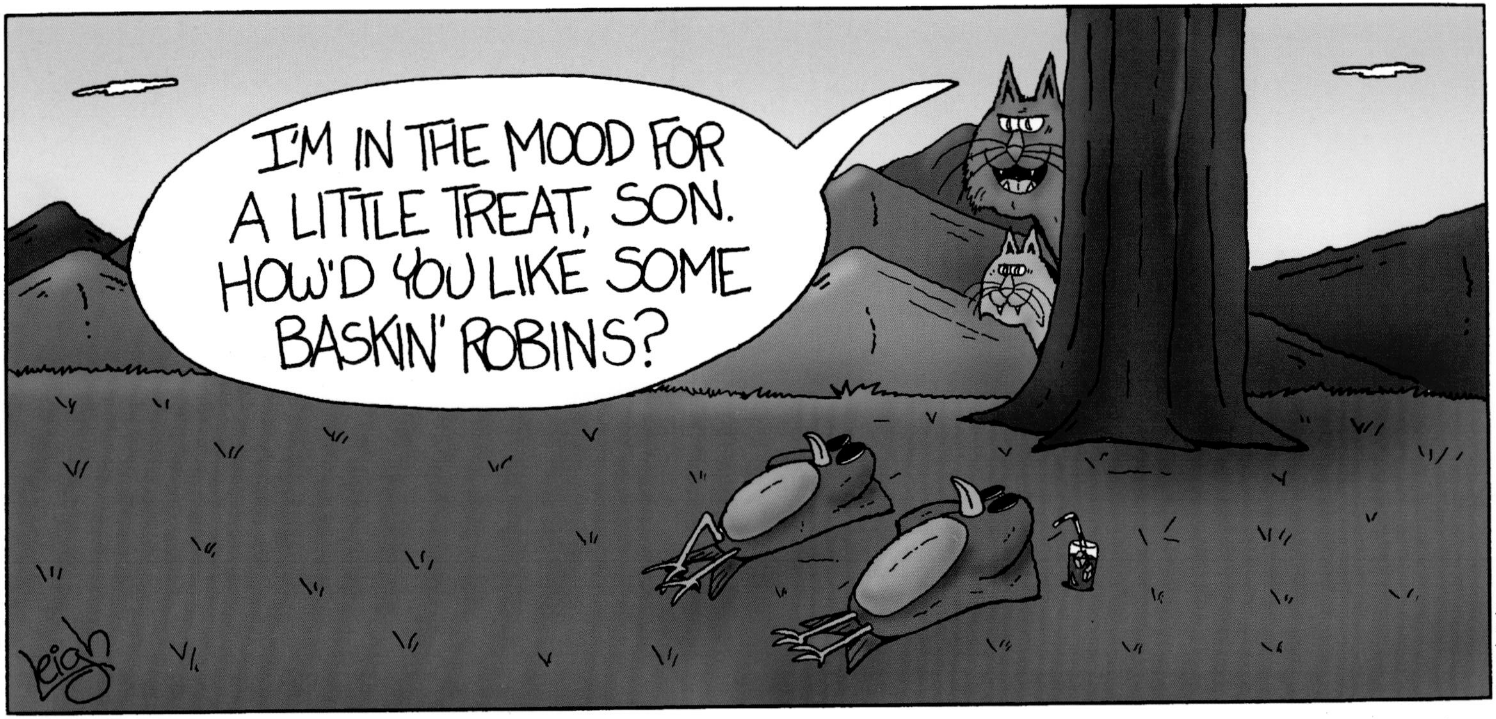
I'M IN THE MOOD FOR A LITTLE TREAT, SON. HOW'D YOU LIKE SOME BASKIN' ROBINS?
leigh

About the Author

Leigh Rubin took his first steps on the path to cartoon success by creating a publishing company and distributing his own greeting cards. Rubes Publications, was established in 1979, and also published the popular Notable Quotes in 1981. Rubes®, in the form that cartoon aficionados now know it, began appearing in newspapers in 1984. The first paperback collection of Rubes® was published in late 1988 by G.P. Putnam & Sons. His most recent series of books include *The Wild Life of Dogs, Pets, Cows* and *Farm Animals*. Originally self-syndicated, Rubes® is now distributed by Creators Syndicate, Inc. to more than 400 newspapers worldwide. As one of the most popular single-panel cartoons, Rubes® is a regular feature in SkyWest's *United Express* and *Delta Connections* magazines, and appears in such major daily metropolitan papers as the *San Diego Union Tribune*, the *Rochester Democrat and Chronicle*, the *Winnipeg Free Press*, the *Washington Times*, the *Houston Chronicle*, the *Orange County Register* and the *Los Angeles Daily News*.

Other books by Leigh Rubin

The Wild Life of Dogs

The Wild Life of Pets

The Wild Life of Cows

The Wild Life of Farm Animals

Rubes® Bible Cartoons

Rubes® Then and Now

Calves Can Be So Cruel

Rubes®

Notable Quotes

Encore!

Amusing Arrangements

Sharks are People Too!